GATHERINGS

Jan Scott & Julie Van Rosendaal

GATHERINGS

BRINGING PEOPLE TOGETHER with FOOD

whitecap

Whitecap Books is known for its expertise in the cookbook market, and has produced some of the most innovative and familiar titles found in kitchens across North America. Visit our website at www.whitecap.ca.

EDITOR Steph Hill
DESIGNER Andrew Bagatella
ILLUSTRATOR Steph Hill
FOOD STYLISTS AND PHOTOGRAPHERS Julie Van Rosendaal and Jan Scott
PROOFREADER Patrick Geraghty

Printed in Canada

Library and Archives Canada Cataloguing in Publication

Van Rosendaal, Julie, 1970-, author
    Gatherings : bringing people together with food / Julie
van Rosendaal & Jan Scott.

ISBN 978-1-77050-226-0 (pbk.)

    1. Cooking. 2. Entertaining. 3. Cookbooks. I. Scott, Jan, 1976-, author II. Title.

TX731.V36 2014   642'.4   C2014-903216-1

The publisher acknowledges the financial support of the Government of Canada through the Canada Book Fund (CBF) and the Province of British Columbia through the Book Publishing Tax Credit.

20 19 18 17 16 15 14   1 2 3 4 5 6 7

To our blog readers, who gather in our

virtual space every day to share recipes and

ideas that collectively bring us together.

CONTENTS

INTRODUCTION

LIFE REVOLVES AROUND gatherings. People are naturally drawn together both to work and play, and most gatherings—or at least the best ones—revolve around food.

Food is our common denominator—it brings people together to celebrate, to comfort, to nourish and entertain in every country in the world. We connect around the table like nowhere else, whether it's a rushed weekday breakfast or an elaborate Sunday supper with extended family; it doesn't have to be a special occasion to count. While food plays a major role in most celebratory events—parties and holidays and such—it can itself be a reason to gather. We are constantly presented with opportunities to get together for bits of social bonding, and while restaurants and coffee shops are booming and bustling, home entertaining has seen a slow demise over the decades since its heyday in the fifties and sixties.

Cooking is as popular as ever—we're watching it on television, devouring food blogs, buying more cookbooks (thanks!) and yes, feeding ourselves and each other. Food (and the sharing of it) brings comfort and joy, and yet too many home cooks are easily overwhelmed by the idea of inviting people into their own kitchens and dining rooms, as if making food and actually serving it to people were two different challenges. This is why Jan and I, who have regular coffee and tea meetings via Skype (with her in Toronto and me in Calgary) to toss around ideas and talk about food in general, decided to write a book that helps ease the pressure of both formal and informal gatherings.

We've provided approachable ideas for all kinds of get-togethers, from fancy meals to weeknight dinners, old-school kids' birthday parties at home, and of course big seasonal feasts. These are the parts of our days, weeks and years we love best, and it's a shame to let pressure or performance anxiety take some of that pleasure away.

Jan's background as an event planner for a Toronto catering company meant that I could refer to her for reminders on how many appetizers or bottles of wine might be needed to feed large groups of people, and she's a fountain of ideas when it comes to easy-to-serve food recommendations, approachable table decorating suggestions (not my forte!) and original birthday party ideas. Working in the food world (and growing up with a Mom who liked to have a house full of people), I've fed more than my share of large groups, and I even had my own catering business for years before I started writing cookbooks. So the two of us figured we'd try to inspire people to bring the party back home. In these pages we've collected some of the best reasons to gather, and rounded up recipes and menus we think are a good fit, along with entertaining tips (including quantities—we've done the math!) and serving ideas that should make it easier to be a guest at your own party. Hopefully it just might inspire you to gather more people around your table, because, as they say, it's not what's on the table that matters, it's who's in the chairs (though gatherings are even more enjoyable when what's on the table is delicious and hasn't caused you a nervous breakdown getting there).

Cheers—to some great gatherings!

Julie and Jan

JAN'S GATHERINGS MANIFESTO: RULES FOR EASY ENTERTAINING

From years of working as a professional event planner and food writer specializing in parties and simple entertaining (not to mention hosting plenty of family-focused gatherings in my own home), I've culled a basic list of rules that I try to apply to most of my get-togethers. When my ideas become bigger than my budget or available time, I often refer back to this list in an effort to remind myself that less is usually more, and a party doesn't have to be fancy in order to be fabulous. A relaxed host who has fun is one of the most important ingredients to any party's success.—JS

THE FOOD

- It's almost always more fun to serve food family-style than to have courses plated and presented to your guests.

- Always try to plan a meal where most of the menu items can be made in advance.

- Include at least one cold or room temperature item on the menu as they are often easier to prepare than hot foods.

- Prepare a DIY *anything*. It can be a taco bar, burger bar, bruschetta bar, potato salad bar, ice cream sundae bar or even just a regular old booze bar. Just set out the components and let your guests help themselves. It's fun, interactive and it works for picky eaters and those with dietary restrictions. Plus, it's easy to execute.

- Don't try any new recipes the day of your party. Instead, make foods that are familiar, simple and uncomplicated.

- Keep cookie dough and ice cream in your freezer at all times. When impromptu guests pop by you'll be able to make homemade ice cream sandwiches for dessert.

- Use plenty of seasonal produce in your menu. It's inexpensive, tastes great and looks fantastic on the plate.

- When in doubt make pulled pork, and serve it with coleslaw, pickles, potato chips and crusty buns. This menu will disappoint very few people.

- If your friends ask whether or not they can bring something, let them. Wine is always a good option, as is dessert (if you don't already have something planned), or suggest a simple salad, which will be easy to assemble.

- Don't overthink the menu. Go with your instincts—they are almost always right.

- Many foods require a resting time when they come out of the oven; consider that detail in your planning and preparation.

- Serve sparkling water—it adds a celebratory feel to any dinner party.

- As a shortcut, consider assembling prepared food instead of cooking it. There are lots of great ways to feed your friends without spending two full days in the kitchen.

- Don't hesitate to skip the fancy dessert. Serving something simple like store-bought ice cream, homemade crunchy cookies or hot coffee can go a long way and will delight most people.

- When hosting a cocktail party stay clear of appetizers that require two hands. Your guests will need one hand for food and one for a drink.

- Most salads need something cheesy or something crunchy, or both. Remember that and you'll have great success serving one to your guests.

- Banish the full bar. Everyone is a cocktail connoisseur these days, but being an expert requires a well-stocked bar with a laundry list of necessary supplies. Serve wine and beer instead, with maybe one specialty cocktail or a holiday punch (which can also double as a centerpiece) and leave it at that.

- Speaking of wine, for ease and economics, keep your selection to one white and one red variety.

- For optimum taste and texture, let your cheese sit at room temperature for at least one hour before serving.

THE GUESTS

- Don't be afraid to invite people over for a casual weeknight dinner instead of a big weekend bash. It's sometimes easier to coordinate guests if you don't have your gathering on the weekend.

- Weekend breakfasts and brunches are a good alternative to a Saturday night dinners, especially when kids are involved.

- Make your guests feel welcome and special. Spoil them and let them know you were thinking of them when you planned your get-together by focusing on the small details that make them feel comfortable.

- When the first guests arrive they should feel as if the party is in full swing; the music should be on and the scent of food should be wafting from the kitchen as you greet them at the door with a drink in your hand.

THE HOUSE

- Don't place scented candles on the dinner table, but rather let the food fill the room with a pleasing aroma. Do feel free to place them in the bathroom, family room or front hall, if you like.

- Play fun music! It fills in the gaps in conversation and creates atmosphere.

- Everyone looks good with a little lighting. Whether you use votive candles, tiki torches, fairy lights or patio lanterns, add a little extra glow to your dinner table.

- Don't feel compelled to clean your entire house before guests come over, but do focus on three main areas: the bathroom (close the shower curtain, clean the sink, empty the garbage and put the toilet seat down), the living room (tidy surfaces, put away throw blankets, tuck toys away, vacuum) and the kitchen (wipe and clear countertops, empty the dishwasher, take out the garbage and recycling).

- It's perfectly acceptable to use mismatched dishes and serving items. A contrasting collection of items can add charm to any table setting.

- Feel free to get creative with your seating arrangements by using round and square tables whenever possible. They're wonderful for conversation, and the surprise set-up will please your guests.

THE PLANNING

- Always, always, plan ahead. Break out the pen and paper and make notes on menu ideas, guests, timing, décor and anything else that might be important.

- If you don't have enough plates, glasses and utensils, rent them. Most party supply stores offer inexpensive rentals that can be returned dirty, making your post-party cleanup a cinch.

- If dining outdoors, keep garbage, compost and recycling bins nearby; people will inevitably need one of the three.

- Incorporate a surprise into every gathering. Plan an unexpected game for the kids, serve important people (like your boss) fun finger foods, and break out the fine china and fancy wineglasses for your neighbours, even when it's just a simple soup and sandwich kind of meal.

- Make flower arrangements at least one day in advance so that the blossoms have enough time to open.

- It's always better to serve large amounts of only a few items than small amounts of a lot of different things. Guests will feel comfortable piling the food up on their plate when there's plenty to be eaten, and it's easier on a host to make fewer types of food.

- Relax. A harried hostess can contaminate the entire feel of a party. Remember that any good gathering should always be fun.

WEEKEND *Brunch*

I LOVE BRUNCH. I love making it almost as much as I love eating it. It's a great meal to gather around, and having everyone over in the morning can be easier to coordinate (and easier on the wallet) than trying to organize a multicourse dinner. Brunch often works better for families with kids—no need to hire a babysitter or leave for an early bedtime. Besides, isn't breakfast everyone's favourite meal of the day?

Just like dinner, brunch can be classy or casual, whatever happens to fit. Break out the good china, serve breakfast-inspired hors d'oeuvres (baby biscuits! Soft-boiled quails' eggs! Wee sausage corn dogs in pancake batter!) and load the table with flowers for a birthday or shower celebration, or stay in your PJs, put the coffee on and heat up the waffle iron for a lazy morning with friends and family. If you're hosting, it's easiest to keep the menu simple. Come up with one starring dish, like truly amazing cinnamon buns or homemade eggs Benedict, then fill the table with a fresh fruit salad, bacon or sausage, and something baked, like muffins or scones. (Having them in the oven as your guests arrive will provide the best welcome—there's nothing more appealing than walking into a warm house filled with the aroma of baking.) Put the coffee on, and your morning is made.—JVR

MIXING UP SOME MIMOSAS

A basic mimosa is made up of champagne and orange juice, with anywhere from equal parts to 3:1, respectively. But it doesn't have to be OJ—try pink grapefruit juice, blood orange juice or even lemonade, and fancy it up with pomegranate arils, muddled raspberries, fresh mint or a small scoop of berry or passion fruit sorbet. If real champagne is a little too rich for your budget, any bottle of dry sparkling wine or Cava will do. Ensure both juice and wine are well chilled, and pour them into wine glasses or tall champagne flutes just before serving.

EGGS BENNY ON PARMESAN POTATO WAFFLES

Who needs an English muffin when you can set your eggs Benny atop a crisp, cheesy waffle? It might seem somewhat involved, but once you have all the elements, they're easy to assemble. You can poach the eggs in advance and keep them in cold water in the fridge; they take just seconds to reheat in simmering water on the stove, making it easier to serve large groups at the same time.

WAFFLES

2 cups (500 mL) cold mashed potatoes

2 large eggs

⅓ cup (80 mL) cream or milk

2 Tbsp (30 mL) canola oil or melted butter

½ cup (125 mL) freshly grated Parmesan cheese

½ cup (125 mL) all-purpose flour

¼ tsp (1 mL) baking powder

salt and pepper, to taste

BLENDER HOLLANDAISE

3 large egg yolks

¼ tsp (1 mL) grainy or Dijon mustard

1 Tbsp (15 mL) lemon juice

pinch salt

½ cup (125 mL) butter

6-8 poached eggs

6-8 thin slices of back bacon or smoked salmon (optional)

- In a large bowl, mix together the mashed potatoes, eggs, cream and oil or butter until well blended and smooth. Add the Parmesan cheese, flour, baking powder, salt and pepper and stir until combined.

- Preheat your waffle iron and spray it with a non-stick spray or brush it with oil. Cook 1 large spoonful of batter at a time until steaming stops and the waffles appear golden and crispy.

- To make the hollandaise, put the yolks, mustard, lemon juice and salt into a blender; cover and pulse until blended. Melt the butter on the stovetop or in the microwave until melted and hot. With the blender on high speed, slowly pour the butter through the feed tube; it should start to thicken to the consistency of mayonnaise. Once all the butter has been added, scrape the hollandaise out into a bowl and keep at room temperature until serving time. (Once refrigerated, it will congeal and turn solid.)

- Top waffles with the poached eggs and, if you like, add back bacon or smoked salmon in between. Drizzle generously with hollandaise.

Serves 6–8

ROASTED POTATOES WITH WHITE CHEDDAR

We dubbed this recipe "Tofino poutine" one summer out on the west coast of Vancouver Island, having become hopelessly addicted to the combination of roasted baby new potatoes aged cheddar. We made it almost every day of our vacation—it was perfect for feeding a large extended family, kids and teenagers included. Once finished, it's easy to keep warm in the oven, especially if you need a little extra time to assemble your eggs Benny.

2 lb (1 kg) thin skinned or new potatoes, scrubbed (halved or quartered, if needed)

canola or olive oil, for cooking

salt and freshly ground black pepper

2–3 cups (500–750 mL) grated old white cheddar

- Preheat the oven to 450°F (230°C).

- In a large roasting pan or rimmed baking sheet, spread the potatoes out in a single layer and drizzle generously with oil. Toss about with your hands to coat the potatoes well with oil, and sprinkle them with salt and pepper.

- Roast for 20 minutes, until the potatoes are soft. Remove from the oven and scatter cheddar over top of them; return to the oven for another 20 minutes, stirring once or twice, until golden and crispy. Serve warm.

Serves 6–8

CANDIED MAPLE BROWN SUGAR BACON

How do you make bacon even better? Baked with a sprinkling of brown sugar and freshly ground black pepper it becomes almost praline-like, and the result is totally delicious.

1 lb (500 g) bacon

¼ cup (60 mL) packed brown sugar

2 Tbsp (30 mL) maple syrup

freshly ground black pepper

- Preheat the oven to 400°F (200°C).

- Lay the bacon out in a single layer on a foil-lined rimmed baking sheet, placing the strips close together—they'll shrink as they cook.

- Bake for 15 minutes, until cooked but still rubbery; remove from the oven and sprinkle with brown sugar, maple syrup and pepper. Return to the oven for 5–7 minutes, until the bacon is crisp and the sugar melted. Transfer to paper towels to absorb any excess drippings and serve warm.

Serves 6–8

THE ULTIMATE GOOEY CINNAMON BUNS

It hardly feels like brunch without a batch of freshly baked, gooey cinnamon buns. Whether you're celebrating Easter or Christmas or just want to make an ordinary Saturday extra special, this recipe will do the trick. If you anticipate a busy morning (or just don't have the gumption to bake immediately after waking up), prepare these buns the night before, then cover and refrigerate—this will slow the rise, and in the morning you need only set them on the counter for half an hour in order to take the chill off before sliding them into the oven to bake.

DOUGH

½ cup (125 mL) warm water

1 Tbsp (15 mL) active dry yeast

½ cup (125 mL) sugar

1 cup (250 mL) milk, warmed

2 large eggs

5 cups (1.25 L) all-purpose flour

½ cup (125 mL) butter, at room temperature

1 tsp (5 mL) salt

GOO

½ cup (125 mL) butter

1 cup (250 mL) packed brown sugar

⅓ cup (80 mL) Roger's or Lyle's Golden syrup, corn syrup or honey

¼ cup (60 mL) water

1 cup (250 mL) pecan halves (optional)

INGREDIENTS CONTINUE . . .

- To make the dough, put warm water in a large bowl (or the bowl of your stand mixer) and sprinkle it with the yeast and a pinch of the sugar. Let stand 5 minutes, or until foamy. (If it doesn't foam, toss it and buy fresh yeast.)

- In a small bowl, mix the warm milk and eggs together with a fork. Add to the yeast mixture along with 3 cups (750 mL) of the flour and the remaining sugar; mix until well blended and sticky.

- Add the butter, salt and remaining flour and stir or beat with the dough hook attachment of your stand mixer until you have a soft, sticky dough. Knead for about 8 minutes, until smooth and elastic. It will still be slightly tacky.

- Place the dough back in the bowl, cover with a tea towel and let it rise in a warm place for 1 hour, or until doubled in bulk.

- Meanwhile, make the goo: Combine the butter, brown sugar, syrup and water in a small saucepan and bring to a simmer, stirring until the butter is melted. Divide between 2 buttered pie plates, two 9-inch (23 cm) cake pans or two 8 × 8-inch (20 × 20 cm) pans, pouring it over the bottom. If you like, scatter with pecan halves.

METHOD CONTINUES . . .

THE ULTIMATE GOOEY CINNAMON BUNS (CONTINUED)

FILLING

¼ cup (60 mL) butter, melted

1 cup (250 mL) packed dark brown sugar

2 tsp (10 mL) cinnamon (approximately)

- To make the buns, divide the dough in half and, on a lightly floured surface, roll each half into a rectangle that's about 10 × 15-inches (25 × 38 cm) or even slightly bigger, even and about ¼-inch (0.6 cm) thick. Brush each piece with half the melted butter and scatter with brown sugar; evenly distribute the sugar with your hand. Sprinkle with cinnamon.

- Starting on a long side, roll the dough up into a log and, using a serrated knife, cut it crosswise into thirds. Cut each of those 3 log-shaped pieces into thirds again—you should end up with 9 even pieces.

- Place the 9 pieces into the pans, cut side facing up, with one bun in the middle and the rest around it, or in the case of a square pan, in 3 rows of 3. Cover with a tea towel and let rise for another hour, until doubled in bulk. (If you're making them the night before, cover and place in the fridge for a slow rise; take them out and leave them on the countertop for 30 minutes or so before baking.)

- When you're ready to bake, preheat the oven to 350°F (175°C). Put a baking sheet on the rack underneath (to catch any drips) and bake for 30–40 minutes, until they turn a deep golden. Let cool for 5–10 minutes, but invert onto a plate while still warm. (If you wait too long and they get stuck in the pan, slide back into a hot oven to rewarm the goo, then try again.) Eat warm.

Makes 1½ dozen cinnamon buns

BRUNCH PUNCH

A couple pitchers or a big bowlful of punch makes bevvies easy. Kids (and anyone not drinking alcohol) can drink it straight, and you can set a bottle of sparkling wine alongside for those who want theirs a little boozy. The frozen apple juice ring keeps it cold and the fruit suspended without watering your punch down.

4 cups (1 L) apple or orange juice

apple slices, orange slices, lemon slices and fresh or frozen cranberries

one 12 oz (355 mL) can orange juice or lemonade concentrate

two 12 oz (355 mL) cans water

4 cups (1 L) cranberry juice

4 cups (1 L) ginger ale, soda water or sparkling wine, for serving

- Pour the apple juice into a Bundt pan or ring mould; add sliced apples, oranges, lemons and a handful of cranberries and freeze until solid.

- Combine the remaining ingredients in a punch bowl, except for the ginger ale, soda or sparkling wine. Gently add the frozen apple juice ring.

- Add about 4 cups (1 L) of the ginger ale or soda or a bottle of wine right to the punchbowl, or leave aside as options; guests can half fill their cup, then top it up with as much bubbly as they like.

Serves about 20

SIMPLE FLAVOURED SYRUP

Starbucks is on to something with those convenient bottles of flavoured syrups, it provides the ability to customize everything from iced tea to your morning latte. Fortunately, simple syrups are easy to make at home, too. Simple syrup got its name for a reason: equal parts sugar and water are simmered until the sugar dissolves, and that's it—add some loose tea or slices of fresh ginger and you have a flavoured syrup. Once cooled, simple syrup keeps for ages in the fridge and can be used to make homemade sodas (just add fizzy water and a scoop of ice cream for an authentic float), and flavour cocktails, as well as to infuse Prosecco and lemonade and to make coffee and hot chocolate more interesting. It's nice to have a few bottles at the bar, or to set out with sparkling water for DIY sodas for the kids.

1 cup (250 mL) sugar

1 cup (250 mL) water

(you can use any quantity of sugar and water, so long as you use the same amount of each.)

YOUR CHOICE OF FLAVOURINGS

thinly sliced fresh ginger

a handful of fresh mint leaves

1 vanilla bean, split lengthwise with the tip of a knife

grated zest of an orange or lemon

1 Tbsp (15 mL) loose tea leaves

a couple cinnamon sticks

a few sprigs of fresh rosemary or basil

a small handful of fresh lavender

- Bring the sugar and water to a simmer in a medium saucepan, stirring until the sugar is dissolved. Add your flavouring of choice and simmer for a few minutes, then remove from heat and let cool—the syrup will steep as it cools, intensifying in flavour.

- Pour the syrup through a strainer or sieve into a jar, cover and store in the fridge for up to a few months.

Makes about 1½ cups (375 mL)

Showers

I ABSOLUTELY LOVE the custom of celebrating life's biggest events—like a wedding or a new baby—with a gathering of friends who are free to ooh and aaah over the guest of honour and the gifts, while enjoying a simply prepared menu peppered with a personal touch or two.

Entertaining etiquette states that a mother, mother-in-law or sister should not throw a shower since it might appear as though they are petitioning for gifts. With no disrespect intended to the etiquette experts, I'm inclined to heartily disagree with their thoughts on this matter. I threw my sister's baby shower, my mother was in charge of mine, and weddings were no different—all of which worked out perfectly. Of course, there are plenty of other factors to take into consideration, like cultural traditions, or where the shower is being held, or who to invite (if it's a wedding shower, you really should only include those who are also being asked to the wedding). With that in mind, deciding who will be in charge of an event isn't always as cut and dried as some might think. And it seems silly to put limitations on who can host a gathering that celebrates a happy future.

Regardless, if you happen to be in charge of one of these events, you are in luck because they are among the easiest to execute. The timeframe is usually fixed (two to three hours in length), the menu is often simple (light and fresh) and the format lends itself well to having fun, especially if there are games involved. Finger foods might be more traditional, but I like the idea of serving a light lunch—something substantial, yet simple, and comprised entirely of items that can be prepared in advance of the guests arriving.—JS

GET YOUR GAME ON

When planning games and activities for a shower the options are endless, but there are two that always seem to be a hit with the crowd. For a baby shower, request that each guest bring a photo of themselves as a baby, and that everyone in the room try to match the baby photos to the guest. The game can last for the duration of the shower, and it encourages lots of mingling as friends try to decide which face looks most familiar.

Wedding showers can be equally as enjoyable, and who can resist a rousing home-version of "The Newlywed Game"? Before the shower, have someone interview the groom and ask him specific questions about the bride, their dating history and general facts about their relationship. Then, at the shower, ask the bride the same questions and see how many she can answer correctly. If you have the equipment, record the groom sharing his answers, and play them at the party after the bride offers her responses to the questions, allowing the whole room to participate in the fun. Whatever games you do decide to play, all of them should ensure that the guest of honour is never embarrassed, and that she leaves the shower feeling special, and most of all, loved.

MAPLE SOY SALMON WITH MUSTARD DILL SAUCE

Salmon is one of the quickest cooking proteins you can prepare, and this recipe is wonderful whether served straight from the oven or at room temperature.

2 Tbsp (30 mL) packed brown sugar

2 Tbsp (30 mL) pure maple syrup

2 Tbsp (30 mL) olive oil

2 Tbsp (30 mL) soy sauce

2 Tbsp (30 mL) lime juice

1 clove garlic, minced

one 3 lb (1.4 kg) side of salmon or eight 6 oz (175 g) filets, deboned, skin on

salt and pepper

Mustard Dill Sauce (below)

- Combine the brown sugar, maple syrup, olive oil, soy sauce, lime juice and garlic in a small saucepan and bring to a simmer over medium-high heat, cooking until thick and syrupy.

- Preheat the oven to 450°F (230°C). Place the salmon, skin side down, on a rimmed baking sheet. Pat flesh dry with a paper towel and season with salt and pepper. Bake for 5 minutes.

- Using a pastry brush, cover the salmon with a thick layer of the glaze. Return to the oven and cook for an additional 7–10 minutes (3–5 for filets), or until the salmon turns opaque and white juices appear. Remove from the oven, brush with another coat of the glaze and let it sit for 5 minutes. Cut crosswise into pieces and serve with Mustard Dill Sauce.

Serves 8

MUSTARD DILL SAUCE

1 cup (250 mL) sour cream or plain yogurt

2 Tbsp (30 mL) lemon juice

2 Tbsp (30 mL) grainy or regular Dijon mustard

3 Tbsp (45 mL) mayonnaise

2–3 Tbsp (30–45 mL) chopped fresh dill

¾ tsp (4 mL) salt

½ tsp (2.5 mL) pepper

This simple sauce can be made up to two days in advance and stored in the fridge until needed.

- Combine all of the ingredients in a small bowl and stir well.

Makes 1½ cups (375 mL)

LEMON, FETA AND ORZO SALAD

I like using orzo in my salads because it fits nicely on a spoon, unlike other larger pastas which can be unwieldy to eat. Although it looks like rice, this quick-cooking and inexpensive ingredient can be found in the pasta aisle of most major grocery stores.

¾ lb (375 g) orzo pasta

½ cup (125 mL) freshly squeezed lemon juice (about 3 lemons)

½ cup (125 mL) good quality olive oil

1 tsp (5 mL) salt

1 tsp (5 mL) freshly ground black pepper

2 cups (500 mL) cherry or grape tomatoes, halved

½ cup (125 mL) minced green onions (white and light green parts only)

1 English cucumber, medium-diced

½ cup (125 mL) diced red onion

1 cup (250 mL) chopped fresh basil

1 cup (250 mL) chopped flat-leaf parsley

¾ lb (375 g) feta cheese, crumbled

- Bring a large pot of salted water to a boil. Add the orzo, reduce the heat to medium and cook as per package directions, or until the pasta is tender and al dente. Drain and pour into a large bowl.

- Whisk together the lemon juice, olive oil, salt and pepper in a small bowl and pour over the warm pasta. Toss well to combine.

- Add the tomatoes, green onions, cucumber, red onion, basil and parsley and stir well. Crumble the feta over the salad and carefully work it in to the other ingredients; taste, and adjust the seasonings if necessary.

- Let the salad sit at room temperature for 1 hour in order for the flavours to incorporate before serving. Alternatively, feel free to refrigerate the salad overnight. If refrigerated, bring back to room temperature and check the seasonings before serving.

PARTY POINTER This salad is incredibly versatile. Feel free to add or substitute sliced black olives, diced red pepper, fresh baby spinach, chopped marinated artichoke hearts or pine nuts into the recipe.

Serves 6

BOURSIN AND SPINACH PALMIERS

With a little help from grocery store favourites like frozen puff pastry, bottled pesto and Boursin cheese, this butterfly-shaped French pastry comes together quickly to create an impressive finger food your guests will love.

¼ cup (60 mL) butter

4 shallots, thinly sliced

2 cups (500 mL) finely chopped mushrooms

6 cups (1.5 L) fresh baby spinach

salt and pepper

all-purpose flour, for sprinkling

2 sheets frozen puff pastry, defrosted

¼ cup (60 mL) pesto

one 5 oz (150 g) pkg Boursin cheese, crumbled

- Melt the butter in a medium skillet over medium heat. Add the shallots and cook until softened, stirring occasionally. Scatter the mushrooms over top and toss to combine until cooking golden brown. Add the spinach and continue cooking, until slightly wilted. Season well with salt and pepper, transfer to a bowl and cool completely.

- Lightly flour a work surface and carefully unfold one sheet of puff pastry. Dust the top with flour and roll the pastry with a rolling pin until it measures 10 × 13 inches (25 × 33 cm).

- Spread half the pesto over the sheet of puff pastry. Top with half the mushroom and spinach mixture and half the crumbled Boursin cheese.

- Starting at one of the short ends of the rectangle, fold the end over halfway to the middle of the pastry. Fold the other side over, and then fold each side in half again so the folded edges come together in the middle. Fold once more so the folded halves are stacked on top of each other. Transfer to a parchment lined baking sheet and repeat steps with the other sheet of puff pastry and the remaining ingredients.

- Cover the baking sheet with parchment paper and chill the pastry in the fridge for 1–3 hours.

- When ready to bake, preheat the oven to 400°F (200°C). Cut the pastry rolls into ¼-inch (0.6 cm) thick slices (about 24 per roll) and place them face up on the baking sheet, spacing them 2 inches (5 cm) apart. Bake for 15–17 minutes, or until puffed and golden brown. Serve warm.

Makes 48 pieces

CRUDITÉ IN CUPS WITH PARSLEY HUMMUS

With food being the focus of so many showers, it's important to prepare something memorable for your guests, and these colourful crudité cups are an excellent hors doeuvre to start with. They can be passed around, or placed on a tray and set in the middle of a table for easy munching.

6 shot glasses, votive candleholders or small Mason jars

2 small Belgian endives, ends trimmed and leaves separated

1 cup (250 mL) green beans, blanched in boiling water for 2 minutes, cooled, drained, trimmed

3 mini cucumbers, ends trimmed and quartered

6 baby orange or yellow carrots, halved lengthwise, green ends trimmed to 1 inch (2.5 cm) above the top of the carrot

1 yellow or orange bell pepper, cored and cut into matchsticks

Parsley Hummus (page 33)

· Using a funnel and small ladle or ice cream scoop, fill each of the glass jars or votive holders with ¼ cup (60 mL) of the Parsley Hummus. Divide the vegetables evenly between the glasses and serve.

Serves 6-12

PARSLEY HUMMUS

1 small bunch parsley (curly or Italian), stems removed, chopped

¼ cup (60 mL) olive oil

one 19 oz (540 mL) can chickpeas, drained

juice of 1 lemon

1 garlic clove (or 1 head roasted garlic)

1 Tbsp (15 mL) sesame oil

pinch salt

· In the bowl of a food processor, pulse the parsley and olive oil until you get a rough sludge. Add the rest of the ingredients and process until the mixture is as smooth as you like it; taste and adjust ingredients to suit your preference.

PARTY POINTER Both the dip and the vegetables can be prepared one day in advance. In fact, hummus tastes even better on the second day than it does on the first, so it's worth planning ahead. Store the hummus in a lidded container in the fridge, and place the vegetables in an airtight container, covered with a piece of paper towel to absorb any excess moisture.

Makes about 2½ cups (625 mL)

FRENCH YOGURT CAKE WITH BLACKBERRIES AND MINT

This one-bowl creation is a staple of French grandmothers everywhere, and once you try it you'll know why. The cake benefits from sitting for a day before serving, making it an ideal make-ahead dessert. Store it at room temperature tightly covered in plastic wrap and add the berries and garnish upon presentation to your guests. Feel free to add a generous dollop of lightly sweetened whipped cream as well. You won't regret it.

BERRIES

2 cups (500 mL) fresh blackberries

1 Tbsp (15 mL) lemon juice

1 Tbsp (15 mL) sugar

CAKE

¾ cup (185 mL) plain Greek yogurt

3 large eggs

1 cup (250 mL) sugar

1 tsp (5 mL) vanilla

1½ cups (750 mL) all-purpose flour

2½ tsp (12.5 mL) baking powder

½ tsp (2.5 mL) salt

½ cup (125 mL) canola or olive oil

GARNISH

2 Tbsp (30 mL) icing sugar

fresh mint leaves

· Combine the blackberries, lemon juice and sugar in a medium bowl and stir gently, so as not to mash up the berries but just lightly coat them. Cover and place in the fridge for up to 2 days or until ready to serve.

· Preheat the oven to 350°F (175°C) and grease a 9-inch (23 cm) springform pan.

· In a medium mixing bowl whisk together the yogurt, eggs, sugar and vanilla. Add the flour, baking powder and salt and stir just until combined. Using a spatula, fold in the oil until you're left with a batter that's thick and shiny.

· Pour the batter into the prepared pan and bake for 35–40 minutes, or until a toothpick inserted into the centre of the cake comes out clean. Allow the cake to cool for 10 minutes before removing it from the pan.

· To serve the cake, lightly dust the top with icing sugar, mound the macerated (or fresh) berries in the centre of the cake and garnish with fresh mint leaves.

Serves 8

"MOM"-OSA

If you're feting an expectant mother, offer her this fun non-alcoholic version of a traditional mimosa. Follow Julie's instructions for making mimosas (Mixing Up Some Mimosas, page 11) and replace the alcohol with sparkling water or seltzer. Garnish with orange slices and fresh strawberries.

PARTY POINTER To make glasses look more festive, dip the rims in lime juice and cover with a band of fine sanding sugar about 1-inch (2.5 cm) wide.

SIMPLE PARTY PUNCH

This popular party punch is non-alcoholic, making it perfect for serving at a baby shower or to a group of kids.

two 12 oz (355 mL) cans frozen orange juice concentrate, thawed

one 12 oz (355 mL) can frozen cran-berry juice, thawed

one 12 oz (355 mL) 1 can frozen limeade, thawed

4 cups (1 L) club soda

lime slices, orange segments and fresh or frozen cranberries, for garnish

· Place all of the ingredients in a punch bowl and stir to combine. Add ice and serve.

Makes 10 cups (2½ L)

COFFEE & Doughnuts

New Orleans-Style Sugared Beignets
(and Mini Doughnuts) 41

Maple-Glazed Sour Cream Doughnuts 42

Homemade Churros 45

Apple or Pear Fritters 47

Drinking Chocolate 48

ONE OF OUR family's most memorable get-togethers happened spur-of-the-moment. One Saturday morning in late winter I was up early, as usual, with our young son, and knew that some of our neighbours would be awake earlier than they'd like for similar reasons. I sent a few emails and texts out, suggesting that anyone in need of caffeine and carbs stop by our place later that morning, rather than waiting to cross paths at the coffee shop. I mixed up batches of yeast-raised and cake doughnut dough to roll and cook up throughout the morning as friends came and went. Their toddlers were ecstatic at the array of sprinkled doughnuts and warm cinnamon-sugared doughnut holes which they tossed themselves and carried home in paper lunch bags.

My husband Mike played barista, brewing up coffee and tea we served out of our everyday mugs while the grown-ups visited and commiserated, the kids played and a good time was had by all. No planning required.—JVR

NEW ORLEANS-STYLE SUGARED BEIGNETS (AND MINI DOUGHNUTS)

I live half a block from the offices of a few magazines I write for, and often run into staff parking their cars on my street. I used to joke that I should sit out on my step and hand out muffins in the morning, until one morning I did! I hauled a small table out front and plugged in my wee deep fryer, and cooked up hot sugared beignets in the snow. A beignet, by the way, is a square fritter famously made in the French Quarter of New Orleans; the same dough can be rolled and cut into mini doughnuts using a shot glass and a straw.

1½ cups (375 mL) warm water

⅓ cup (80 mL) sugar

2 tsp (10 mL) active dry yeast

1 cup (250 mL) milk

2 large eggs

2 tsp (10 mL) vanilla

7½ cups (1.85 L) all-purpose flour

¼ cup (60 mL) butter, softened

1 tsp (5 mL) salt

canola oil, for frying

lots of icing sugar

- Put the water in a large bowl and sprinkle a pinch of the sugar and the yeast over top; let sit for 5 minutes. If it's not foamy, toss it and buy new yeast.

- In a small bowl, whisk together the milk, eggs and vanilla. Add to the yeast mixture along with 3 cups (750 mL) of the flour, the remaining sugar, the butter and salt. Stir to combine. Gradually add another 4 cups (1 L) of flour, stirring (or letting your dough hook do the work) until you have a sticky dough. If it's not too sticky to knead, knead it on a floured surface or with the dough hook; if it's still pretty sticky, add another ½ cup (125 mL) flour. Knead until it's smooth and elastic, yet still tacky.

- Put the dough into an oiled bowl, cover with a tea towel and let rise for 1½–2 hours.

- When you're ready to cook, heat a couple inches of oil in a deep-fryer or heavy saucepan until hot, but not smoking (about 350°F [175°C]).

- Roll the dough out about ½-inch (1 cm) thick and cut into 1–2-inch (2.5–5 cm) squares with a knife. Carefully drop a few at a time into the hot oil without crowding it (cooking too many at a time will bring the temperature of the oil down) and cook until golden on both sides, carefully flipping with tongs as necessary. Transfer to paper towels to drain and cool, then douse in powdered sugar.

Makes about 4 dozen beignets

MAPLE-GLAZED SOUR CREAM DOUGHNUTS

The dough for these rich sour cream cake doughnuts is quick to stir together and requires no rising. If you like, skip the doughnuts altogether and drop small spoonfuls of the dough into the oil to make fritters or doughnut holes.

DOUGHNUTS

1 cup (250 mL) sugar

2 large eggs

⅓ cup (80 mL) canola oil or melted butter

1 tsp (5 mL) maple or vanilla extract

3½ cups (875 mL) all purpose flour

1 Tbsp (15 mL) baking powder

½ tsp (2.5 mL) baking soda

½ tsp (2.5 mL) salt

1 cup (250 mL) sour cream

GLAZE

2 cups (500 mL) icing sugar

3 Tbsp (45 mL) half & half or heavy cream

2 Tbsp (30 mL) pure maple syrup

canola oil, for frying

· In a large bowl, beat the sugar and eggs until pale and light. Beat in the oil and maple extract. In a small bowl, stir together the flour, baking powder, baking soda and salt. Add to the sugar mixture in three additions, alternating with the sour cream in two additions. Mix just until combined after each.

· In a heavy pot, heat a couple inches of oil over medium-high heat until it reaches about 375°F (190°C). (Alternatively, heat oil in a deep fryer.) Pat the dough on a lightly floured surface to about ½-inch (1 cm) thick and cut into rounds with a doughnut cutter if you have one, otherwise cut the dough with a round cookie cutter or glass rim, cutting out the middle using a shot glass or smaller round cutter (alternately you can poke a hole with a chopstick and stretch it out with your finger). Gently fry a few at a time, without crowding the pot, flipping with tongs as necessary until deep golden brown. Transfer to paper towels to absorb the oil. Meanwhile, whisk together the icing sugar, cream and maple syrup for the glaze. Drizzle over cooked doughnuts while they're still warm.

Makes about 1½ dozen doughnuts, plus some doughnut holes

HOMEMADE CHURROS

Knowing how to make churros will come in handy no matter what kind of gathering you're planning; a warm batch, doused in cinnamon-sugar, will make everyone very happy. These churros are made with a simple choux pastry, which is generally used to make cream puffs, then squeezed into hot oil using a pastry bag with a star tip (which gives the churros their trademark ridges). Serve warm, with hot drinking chocolate for dunking.

1 cup (250 mL) milk or water

¼ cup (60 mL) butter

2 tsp (10 mL) sugar

¼ tsp (1 mL) salt

1 cup (250 mL) all-purpose flour

4 large eggs

canola oil, for frying

2 tsp (10 mL) cinnamon

1 cup (250 mL) sugar

- In a medium saucepan, bring the milk, butter, sugar and salt to a simmer. Reduce the heat to medium-low, add the flour and stir vigorously by hand until the dough comes together in a smooth ball that cleans the sides of the pot. Transfer to a bowl and let cool for about 10 minutes.

- Using an electric mixer, beat in the eggs one at a time. You'll end up with a sort of smooth, shiny, sticky batter that's thicker than pancake batter but thinner than cookie dough. If you like, you can let it sit at room temperature for 1 hour, or refrigerate for up to 24 hours, until you're ready for it.

- When you're ready to cook your churros, heat a couple inches of canola oil in a pot until the oil is hot but not smoking. Test to see if it's ready by dipping a bit of bread in—it should bubble and sizzle around the bread. Spoon the batter into a pastry bag fitted with a large star tip and squeeze a few inches at a time into the oil, nudging the batter off with a knife. Don't crowd the pot—cook maybe 3 or 4 at a time, flipping them as necessary until they turn golden. They should take a few minutes to cook—test to make sure they are cooked through (if they brown too quickly they might not be, in which case just turn the heat down). Transfer to paper towels to absorb any excess oil.

- In a shallow bowl, combine the cinnamon and sugar. Roll the churros around in it to coat them well while they are still warm. Eat.

Makes a few dozen, depending on individual length

APPLE OR PEAR FRITTERS

Chopped apples and pears make for divine fritters, especially in the fall. These fritters are rough and rustic, dropped by the spoonful into oil to cook, saving the step of rolling and cutting. Keep them small so that they cook through to the middle without darkening too much on the outside, then douse the nubbly golden fritters in icing sugar or cinnamon-sugar while they're still warm.

2 cups (500 mL) all-purpose flour

¼ cup (60 mL) sugar

1 Tbsp (15 mL) baking powder

2 tsp (10 mL) cinnamon

¼ tsp (1 mL) salt

1 cup (250 mL) milk

2 large eggs

3 apples, roughly chopped

canola oil, for frying

icing sugar or cinnamon-sugar, for dusting

- In a large bowl, whisk together the flour, sugar, baking powder, cinnamon and salt. In a small bowl, whisk together the milk and eggs; add to the dry ingredients and stir just until combined. Stir in the apples.

- In a heavy saucepan or small pot, heat a couple inches of oil over medium-high heat until hot but not smoking; drop batter carefully by the small spoonful into the oil and cook, flipping as necessary until golden all over. Remove with tongs or a slotted spoon and place on paper towels.

- Sprinkle icing sugar or cinnamon sugar generously over top while the fritters are still warm.

Makes lots

DRINKING CHOCOLATE

Thick, rich drinking chocolate is a perfect alternative to coffee for kids or for anyone who prefers a more indulgent dunk.

¼ cup (60 mL) sugar

¼ cup (60 mL) cocoa

3 cups (750 mL) milk, 2% or whole

¼–½ cup (60–125 mL) chopped dark chocolate

· In a medium saucepan, whisk together the sugar and cocoa to get rid of any lumps. Set over medium-high heat and whisk in the milk; bring to a simmer, whisking well. Remove from heat and add the chocolate. Let stand for 1 minute, then whisk until smooth. Serve hot.

Serves 4

PIE Party

ONE OF THE best parties I ever threw was such a hit that it made the pages of the *Ladies' Home Journal* after editors read about it on my blog. It was a pie potluck—a simple call out to friends to come over and bring a pie. Who doesn't love pie?

Potlucks are a great way to take the pressure off of entertaining, but a specific theme makes things even easier. In this instance the theme was simply: come over, bring pie. Everyone was excited to bake their favourite pie, or to pick one up from their favourite bakery. Some (many) worried that if I didn't assign a specific type of pie, or let people dibs their planned pie then, somehow, we'd wind up with a dozen apple pies. But the essence of a potluck is the luck of the draw, isn't it? In the end, I don't think apple pie even made an appearance, unless you count the apple-pear galette with cheddar cheese crust that I made myself. Every pie was different.

The party took place on a Saturday afternoon—is there a better sight than friends arriving at your door with warm pies wrapped in tea towels? I doubt it. There was a bumbleberry pie and Saskatoon pie, a stunning peach pie with a lattice top, and chocolate chip cookie dough pie with cookie dough baked right into the crust. Jenna made her very first pecan pie, Andy brought a ginger pear galette with Greek yogurt for spooning over top, and Darrel and Corrine brought a graham cracker crusted no-bake cheesecake pie topped with sliced peaches, blueberries and wee strawberries from their backyard. Lauren's peach-berry pie was gluten-free, made with almond, sweet rice and millet flours, and Catharine brought peach-plum galettes sprinkled with sugar and rubbed with fresh mint. In the end there happened to be no savoury pies, but if there had been I'm sure they could have been contenders—meat pies or veggie pies or quiche, even.

Between the people and the pies, the whipped cream, sunshine and bubbly drinks (Prosecco, sangria and mint lemonade), it was a pretty fantastic afternoon. And I'm determined to make it an annual event.—JVR

ALL BUTTER PASTRY

This basic pastry is easy to recreate from memory after you've made it a couple times—it's easily doubled for a double crust pie.

1¼ cups (310 mL) all-purpose flour

¼ tsp (1 mL) salt

½ cup (125 mL) cold butter, cut into pieces

¼–⅓ cup (60–80 mL) cold water

- In a medium bowl or the bowl of a food processor, stir together the flour and salt; add the butter and blend with a pastry cutter or fork, or pulse in the food processor until it's almost blended, with bits of butter left over that are no bigger than the size of a large pea. If you're using a food processor, dump it out into a bowl.

- Add ¼ cup (60 mL) of cold water and stir until the dough comes together; if it's too dry, add a little more water. Shape the dough into a disc, wrap in plastic and refrigerate for 1 hour. (It can be frozen at this point for months.)

- When you're ready to bake, lightly flour the countertop and roll it out ⅛-inch (0.3 cm) thick, then proceed with your recipe.

Makes enough for a single crust pie or about a dozen tarts

HOW TO MAKE HAND PIES

Most pies—with the exception of custard-filled—can be made into small moon-shaped pies you can hold in your hand. To achieve this, simply roll and cut your dough into rounds about 3 or 4 inches (8–10 cm) in diameter, then add a large spoonful of filling and fold the pastry over, crimping the edge to seal. Place on a parchment-lined baking sheet and, if you like, brush the pastry tops with a little milk or cream. Cut a few slits to allow steam to escape and bake at 375 °F (190 °C) for 20 minutes, or until the crust is golden and the filling is bubbly. Transfer to wire racks to cool.

SAUTÉED APPLE PIE

Apple pie is a classic, most often made with raw, sliced apples. Sautéing them first gets rid of some excess moisture, meaning that they won't shrink as much as they bake inside the pie. A hot pan will also caramelize them, adding flavour rather than just steaming them inside of the crust. I learned this technique from the *New York Times,* circa 2001.

FILLING

2 Tbsp (30 mL) butter

2 Tbsp (30 mL) canola oil

4–5 lb apples (8–10 apples), peeled, cored and sliced

2 Tbsp (30 mL) lemon juice

½ cup (125 mL) sugar

3 Tbsp (45 mL) all-purpose flour

1 tsp (5 mL) cinnamon

¼ tsp (1 mL) salt

pastry for a double crust pie (see All Butter Pastry, page 54)

cream, for brushing (optional)

sugar, for sprinkling (optional)

- In a large skillet, heat the butter and oil over medium-high heat. Add the apples and sauté, turning occasionally, for 5–6 minutes, until starting to soften and turn golden. Sprinkle with the lemon juice, sugars, flour, cinnamon and salt and cook for another 2–3 minutes. Set aside to cool slightly.

- Preheat the oven to 400°F (200°C). Divide the pastry into two slightly uneven halves; roll out the larger piece on a lightly floured surface into a 10-inch (25 cm) circle and gently fit into the pie plate. Fill with the cooled apples. Roll out the remaining pastry and cover the filling (or cut into strips to make a lattice top); seal, trim and crimp the edges. Cut several slits in the top to allow steam to escape.

- If you like, brush the top crust with cream and sprinkle with sugar. Bake for about 40 minutes, until golden. Serve warm, at room temperature or cold. Top with ice cream or whipped cream, if desired.

Serves 8

STRAWBERRY-RHUBARB PIE

Strawberry-rhubarb is the ultimate summer pie, though raspberries pair just as well if you have some in your garden and want to sub them in. If the idea of a lattice crust makes you nervous, top your pie with a full crust and cut a few slits in the top to let the steam escape.

pastry for a double crust pie (see All Butter Pastry, page 54)

3–4 cups (750 mL–1 L) chopped fresh rhubarb

3–4 cups (750 mL–1 L) strawberries

½ cup (125 mL) sugar

½ cup (125 mL) packed brown sugar

3 Tbsp (45 mL) cornstarch

milk or cream, for brushing (optional)

sugar, for sprinkling (optional)

- Preheat the oven to 400°F (200°C).

- Divide the pastry into two slightly uneven halves. On a lightly floured surface, roll the bigger piece of pastry out into a 12-inch (30 cm) circle. Drape the pastry over your rolling pin, transfer it to a pie plate and fit it inside, letting the edges hang over.

- Put the rhubarb and strawberries in a large bowl. In a smaller bowl, stir together the sugars and cornstarch; add to the fruit and toss gently to combine. Mound into the pie crust.

- Roll the other piece of pastry out into a 10-inch (25 cm) circle and cut into ½-inch (1 cm) strips. Lie half of them in one direction across the pie, leaving about half an inch between them. Starting at one side, fold back all but the first, and weave the remaining strips in the opposite direction, laying them under and over alternating strips. Pinch the edges to seal, then trim and crimp them. If you like, brush the top of the pie with milk or cream, and sprinkle with sugar.

- Bake for 20 minutes, then reduce the oven temperature to 350°F (175°C) and bake for another hour, until the pastry is golden and the juices are bubbly. If the crust is browning too quickly, cover the pie loosely with foil. Cool before cutting.

PARTY POINTER You can also bake this pie in a single crust topped with a crumble. To make the crumble, take ½ cup (125 mL) flour, ½ cup (125 mL) brown sugar and ¼ (60 mL) butter and rub together until crumbly. Spread over top the pie and bake as above.

Serves 8

STONE FRUIT AND BERRY GALETTE

For pie-lovers intimidated by the demands of pie-prep (fitting pastry into a pie plate, crimping edges, worrying about shrinkage as the pie bakes) a free-form tart, also known as a galette, is an excellent, stress-free alternative. A rolled-out piece of dough can be wonky, but here it won't matter; place it on a parchment-lined sheet, pile it with fruit, then fold the pastry over to partially enclose it. The more rough and rustic it looks, the better.

pastry for a single crust pie (see All Butter Pastry, page 54)

FILLING

2–3 plums or 1–2 peaches, pitted and sliced

2 cups (500 mL) fresh or frozen blueberries

1 cup (250 mL) fresh or frozen raspberries or blackberries

1 Tbsp (15 mL) lemon juice

½ cup (125 mL) sugar

2 Tbsp (30 mL) all-purpose flour

cream and coarse sugar, for brushing and sprinkling (optional)

- On a lightly floured countertop, roll the pastry out into about a 12-inch (30 cm) circle. Transfer it to a parchment-lined baking sheet and preheat the oven to 375°F (190°C).

- In a large bowl, toss the fruit with the lemon juice. Stir together the sugar and flour and sprinkle over the fruit. Toss to coat and mound into the middle of the pastry, leaving an inch or two uncovered around the edge.

- Fold the edge over in several places, partially enclosing the fruit. If you like, brush the pastry with milk or cream and sprinkle with sugar.

- Bake for 40–45 minutes, until the fruit is bubbly and the crust is golden. Let cool to lukewarm before you cut into it. Serve with ice cream or whipped cream.

Serves 8

FLAVOURED WHIPPED CREAM

Why not give your whipped cream a flavour boost? It's common to add a little vanilla along with a spoonful of sugar, but you could also use other extracts instead—try coconut, maple or mint. Alternative sweeteners, such as dark brown sugar, pure maple syrup or honey, will add a subtle flavour. Or try steeping your cream by bringing it to a simmer with sliced fresh ginger or loose Earl Grey tea; strain through a sieve and chill before whipping.

CECILIA'S NENSHI PIE

This pie was inspired by Calgary mayor Naheed Nenshi's mother's samosa recipe. It's a deliciously different meat pie that's best served with a hefty dollop of chutney. Cecelia was the one to translate those samosas into pie form.

FILLING

canola oil, for cooking

1 lb (500 g) lean ground beef or lamb

1 small onion, finely chopped

1 small jalapeño pepper, seeded and finely minced

2 garlic cloves, crushed

1 tsp (5 mL) grated fresh ginger

4 green onions, finely chopped

½ cup (loosely packed) chopped fresh cilantro (include the stems)

2 tsp (10 mL) lime or lemon juice

½ tsp (2.5 mL) garam masala

½ tsp (2.5 mL) coriander

½ tsp (2.5 mL) cumin

¼ tsp (1 mL) salt

pastry for a single or double crust pie (see All Butter Pastry, page 54), or 1 sheet thawed puff pastry

mango or other fruit chutney, for serving

- In a large, heavy skillet, heat a drizzle of oil over medium-high heat and cook the ground beef or lamb and onion, breaking up any lumps of meat with a spoon until it's no longer pink. As it cooks, add the jalapeño pepper, garlic and ginger. Once cooked, stir in the green onions, cilantro, lime juice, garam masala, coriander, cumin and salt and cook for another minute. Set aside to cool slightly.

- Preheat the oven to 425°F (220°C). On a lightly floured surface, roll the pastry into a 10-inch (25 cm) circle. Fit it into a pie plate or place on a parchment-lined baking sheet. Fill the shell or mound the filling in the middle of the pastry, leaving an inch or so around the edge. If you like, top with a second piece of pastry, then pinch to seal, trimming and crimping the edges. If you're making a galette, fold the pastry over the filling around the edge—it won't cover it completely.

- If you like, brush the top or edge of pastry with beaten egg. Bake for 30 minutes, until golden. Serve warm or at room temperature, with chutney.

Serves 6

HOW TO HOST A PIE PARTY

- Fold some blank cards and leave them on the table with a Sharpie so that everyone can make a sign identifying their pie.

- Have plenty of small plates and forks—plastic will do, but I picked up a ton of mismatched forks from the thrift store and keep them in the basement. I store them in a Mason jar—and put them out that way too.

- If you like, keep a roll of masking tape on hand so that you can stick names on the bottoms of pie plates as the guests arrive—there will be a lot of empty ones at the end of your party, and many will look the same.

- You'll need whipped cream—and vanilla ice cream too. Sweeten your whipped cream with icing sugar, which will help stabilize it a bit.

THE PANTRY Party

T HE FIRST TIME I hosted a holiday cookie exchange I liked it well enough, but not so much that I wanted to repeat the activity year after year. It was great fun to gather some of my favourite people together, but trying to coordinate a date that worked well for everyone was no easy feat. As we all know, the December calendar is mostly chock-a-bloc full by the middle of November.

Instead, I started thinking about how fun it would be to rally everyone at another time of the year. Maybe in February, when the dull days of winter take over, or in the late spring before everyone leaves town for summer vacation. September also held a certain appeal, as canning season is at its peak and jars are being filled with the best of the season's bounty. In fact, the more I thought about it, the more I realized that there are many times of the year that are perfect for gathering together with your friends, and the idea of a holiday exchange quickly morphed into a desire to host a pantry party. If friends can come together to share and swap handmade condiments and baked goods (or store-bought specialties they can't live without) in a relaxed setting, especially during a month that isn't already bursting with commitments and festivities, that might work out better for everyone, host included.

While it is possible to keep this kind of get-together limited to cookies, as is tradition, it's also fun to exchange other types of edibles with friends: a favourite granola or pancake mix, a flavoured boozy beverage, finishing salts or oven-roasted pizza sauce, or even that imported vinegar you just can't live without. Regardless of what you decide to swap, you won't regret having an opportunity to enjoy the company of like-minded bakers, canners, cooks and food makers in a casual setting that requires very little coordination.—JS

HOW TO HOST A PANTRY PARTY

- Choose a date and send invitations via email, evite or Facebook group. While old-fashioned paper and post invites are pretty, electronic communication allows guests to share which pantry items they'll be bringing in order to avoid duplicates, and it provides people with a means of keeping track of how many invitees are coming so that they know how much food is required.

- Keep in mind that while weekends are a great time for hosting parties to entertain a crowd, this gathering is ideal for a casual weeknight get-to-gether with a small group. Guests will appreciate that there isn't a huge time commitment involved.

- Ask guests to bring one food item per person in attendance, plus an extra for sampling if appropriate. This format works well if there are less than 12 people participating. If you're inviting a larger group (15 or more), ask guests to bring 12 items total. Request that guests take only as much as they brought (for example, if someone brings 10 jars of jelly that they leave with 10 new food items). Ask guests to bring a copy of their recipe if the item they are sharing is homemade, and be sure to insist that items being swapped travel well, in order to avoid breakage and spilling on the trip home.

- Set up a long table for guests to put their goods on. Provide a small station fitted with assorted labels and pens in case some of the guests forget to label their items.

- This is one of the easiest gatherings to host since the guests provide most of the food. As the host, provide a simple cheese and cracker tray (see How to Build a Cheese Board, page 255) for nibbling and pairing with any condiments that are available for tasting. Keep small plates and tasting utensils available for sampling the other goods. The host is also in charge of providing the beverages. For an afternoon event, coffee, tea, homemade sodas and hot chocolate (see Drinking Chocolate, page 58) are nice options. For an evening, consider offering wine or Prosecco as well.

ITEMS TO SWAP AT A PANTRY PARTY

Bring any of the following homemade or store-bought items to a pantry swap and your friends are guaranteed to leave the party with armfuls of tasty tokens as a reminder of a good time with great company:

- jam
- jelly
- marmalade
- infused honey
- chutney
- relish
- salsa
- pickles
- pesto
- sauces
- condiments (ketchup, barbecue sauce)
- infused alcohols
- granola
- pancake/baking mixes
- spice blends
- flavoured salts
- cookies and bars
- muffins
- quick breads
- flavoured syrups

CLUMPY PEANUT BUTTER AND HONEY GRANOLA

Peanut butter adds a lovely layer of flavour to the granola without the additional sweetness often found in breakfast cereal recipes. Periodically I like to swap in pure maple syrup for honey, or dried cranberries or cherries for dates.

4 cups (1 L) old-fashioned large flake oats

1 cup (250 mL) sliced almonds

1 cup (250 mL) sweetened shredded coconut

½ tsp (2.5 mL) fine sea salt

½ cup (125 mL) all-natural creamy peanut butter

½ cup (125 mL) honey

1 tsp (5 mL) pure vanilla extract

⅓ cup (80 mL) packed brown sugar

2 Tbsp (30 mL) olive oil

1 egg white, whisked until foamy

1 cup (250 mL) or about 9 Medjool dates, chopped

- Preheat the oven to 300°F (150°C) and line a rimmed baking sheet with parchment paper.

- In a large bowl, mix together the oats, almonds, coconut, and salt.

- In a small saucepan, combine the peanut butter, honey, vanilla, brown sugar and olive oil, and cook over low heat until melted and smooth. Pour over the oat mixture and mix until well combined. Add the egg white and stir again to distribute evenly through the oats.

- Spread the mixture onto the prepared baking sheet and bake for 20 minutes. Remove from the oven and stir, taking care not to break up the clumps, and cook for an additional 10–12 minutes or until slightly golden in colour and crunchy.

- Let cool completely, then break into smaller pieces, if required. Stir in the chopped dates and store in an airtight container for up to 1 week.

Make 6 cups (1.5 kg)

FROM THE KITCHEN OF

Beth
-xo-

GARLIC AND HERB FINISHING SALT

Simple seasoning transforms into something truly amazing when you marry it with a combination of citrus zest, fresh herbs and garlic. Packaged in small glass jars and adorned with a sleek label, this homemade spice instantly becomes a special treat worthy of sharing with friends.

4 cloves garlic

zest of 1 large lemon (about 1–2 teaspoons)

¼ cup (60 mL) fresh rosemary leaves

10 Tbsp (150 mL) kosher salt

- Preheat the oven to 200°F (95°C) and line a rimmed baking sheet with parchment paper.

- Peel the garlic and place in the bowl of a food processor along with the lemon zest, rosemary leaves and two tablespoons of the salt. Blend until the mixture resembles wet sand. Transfer to the baking sheet and toss with the remaining salt.

- Spread the mixture evenly over the pan and bake for 14–16 minutes or until it looks dry. Cool completely and break up any chunks, if necessary. Store in a sealed jar.

Makes 1 scant cup (approximately 240 mL)

BOOZY APPLE BARBECUE SAUCE

This sauce can be preserved, as per the recipe directions, or it can be capped and stored in the fridge for two to three months. Slather it over grilled meats for a fall-inspired twist on a classic condiment.

8 cups (2 L) chopped apples (peeled and cored)

2 cups (500 mL) chopped onions

3 cloves garlic, chopped

one 5½ oz (156 mL) can tomato paste

¾ cup (185 mL) brown sugar

¾ cup (185 mL) apple cider vinegar

½ cup (125 mL) white vinegar

¼ cup (60 mL) whiskey or bourbon

¼ cup (60 mL) Worcestershire sauce

1 tsp (5 mL) salt

2 tsp (10 mL) smoked paprika

- To prepare, boil clean jars in a water bath for 10 minutes to sterilize them; leave them in the hot water until you're ready to fill them. Place the sealing lids and rings in a small saucepan, cover with water and bring to a boil. Leave them in the hot water until ready to use.

- Combine the barbecue sauce ingredients in a large stockpot and bring to a boil. Stir, reduce the heat to medium-low and simmer for 25 minutes, or until the apples are tender. Remove from the stovetop and allow to cool for 5 minutes. Purée the sauce (in batches if necessary) and ladle into hot jars leaving a ½-inch (1 cm) headspace at the top.

- Wipe the rims of the jars thoroughly and remove the sealing lids from the hot water, attaching them to the jars with the rings.

- If preserving, return the jar to the water bath (making sure they are covered by at least 1 inch [2.5 cm] of water) and process for 20 minutes.

- Transfer the jars to a cooling rack or tea towel on the counter and allow them to cool completely while listening for the "pop" to ensure they've sealed properly.

Makes five 1 cup (250 mL) jars

HONEY CARDAMOM BUTTER

Smear this on homemade biscuits, or portion into ½ cup (125 mL) jars and give as a gift along with a warm loaf of homemade banana bread.

1 cup (250 mL) unsalted butter, room temperature

3 Tbsp (45 mL) honey

½ tsp (2.5 mL) vanilla extract

½ tsp (2.5 mL) ground cardamom

pinch of sea salt

- Place the butter in the bowl of an electric mixer with the paddle attachment and beat on low to loosen and fluff it up. Increase the speed to medium and add the honey, vanilla, cardamom and sea salt. Beat until well combined, about 5–6 minutes.

- Transfer to a small glass jar, cover and store in fridge for up to 1 week.

Makes 1 cup (250 mL)

HOMEMADE VANILLA EXTRACT

When producing your own homemade vanilla extract, vodka offers the most neutral flavour, but if you like the idea of adding a little something special try making it with either bourbon or rum. You don't need to purchase a high-proof alcohol for this project, as an inexpensive alcohol will work just as well. If making these for a gift, be sure to let the recipient know how long they need to let their vanilla steep for before using it.

3 vanilla beans

1 cup (250 mL) vodka, bourbon or rum

- Using a sharp paring knife, split the vanilla beans in half lengthwise, leaving 1 inch (2.5 cm) at the top and bottom of each bean uncut.

- Place the vanilla beans in a glass jar with a tight fitting lid and cover with alcohol, making sure the beans are completely submerged in the liquid. Seal the jar tightly and give it a good shake. Store in a dark, cool and dry place for about 2 months, remembering to shake the jar once a week or so.

- To extract the vanilla, remove vanilla beans and decant into a jar. There will be small seed flecks in your extract, but if you prefer a clear liquid you can strain the extract through a coffee filter before packaging in a new bottle. Double or triple as needed.

Makes 1 cup (250 mL)

HOW TO HOST A FREEZER PARTY

In this age of multitasking, why not host a dinner party that not only feeds everyone well and allows for socializing, but also anticipates other meals down the road? Hosting a freezer party is common when anticipating of a new baby's arrival, but let's face it, we all have to eat, and inviting a few friends over to cook is not only an enjoyable way to spend an afternoon, it harkens back to a time when it was common for women to gather and make enormous batches of perogies or ravioli to stock their fridges with—enough to feed their families for weeks—while they caught up on the who and what.

The popularity of pre-prepared meals (as opposed to frozen ones) is evidence of our need to feed our families something resembling home-made food whenever possible, whilst also keeping things convenient. Some address this daily challenge with meal plans; others spend weekends in the kitchen, stashing dinners in the freezer for the upcoming week. But hosting a "dinner" party is my favourite way to spend time with family and friends who also have to eat; it reminds me of Thanksgiving or Christmas, when I get to spend the afternoon in the kitchen with my mom and sisters preparing the big feast. Spending a weekend afternoon chopping vegetables and drinking wine with friends is the ultimate in social multitasking, especially if it means bringing home a handful of dinners and lunches for the week ahead. And really—everyone always ends up in the kitchen at a party anyway; you may as well hand them a knife.

· Don't invite too many people—the phrase "too many cooks in the kitchen" is a cliché for a reason.

· Plan what you're going to make beforehand. Let everyone choose one or two recipes, and have each person bring the primary ingredients for their dish. You should supply the basics, like cooking oil and common spices.

· When choosing what to prepare, any dish with plenty of liquid freezes well, so think soups, stews, chilis and curries.

· Consider cooking methods—having a dish or two simmering on the stovetop (such as soup or chili) and others that don't require heat (such as cookie dough—dessert counts too!) will evenly distribute workspace.

· Assemble casseroles and items like lasagna up to the point of baking, then cover and freeze to bake from frozen.

· Pick up freezer bags and aluminum take-out containers at the dollar store; having something disposable will ensure all your good Tupperware doesn't end up in the freezer.

· Pick up a few bottles of wine, crank up the music and have fun!

KID'S BIRTHDAY *Party*

ASSUMING THAT THE average Canadian mom has at least two children—or maybe more thanks to the largest baby boom since the late 1950s—she will likely be responsible for hosting/arranging more than 30 birthday parties for her children over the course of their childhood. The annual occasion in which our kids cross one more year off their childhood calendar is a cause for celebration, and nothing says "let's party" quite like a birthday bash complete with festive food, crafty decorations and simple party games and activities.

This chapter is dedicated to the creation of a colourful childrens' birthday party that is slightly old-fashioned in its execution, taking place at home with a traditional party menu, homemade birthday cake, handmade party decorations and games that are only limited by what can be imagined. There doesn't need to be a specific theme to guide this type of celebration; instead of using cartoon characters, movies and books to unite the many elements of a party, this humble bash should honour the birthday boy or girl in whatever creative and thoughtful way best represents them.

While it can be difficult to remember, a children's birthday party isn't meant to impress the other parents or family members in attendance. Birthday party planning isn't a competitive sport, despite how it may appear at times, and less is definitely more when it comes to preparing for these parties. Put your focus where your strengths lie and you'll automatically feel at ease about your hosting duties. If you are more interested in assembling handmade decorations than baking a birthday cake, don't hesitate to let someone else supply the sweet treats for you. It's important to remember that your child's birthday is a happy occasion which they look forward to all year long, eager with anticipation to turn another year older. The main focus should be on them and their friends in attendance, not on what you weren't able to accomplish for the party.—JS

THE PARTY SUPPLY CLOSET

The easiest way to prepare for any birthday celebration is to keep a well-stocked party supply closet full of assorted disposable decorations and materials for quick and easy handmade creations. This doesn't have to be a real closet per se, but rather a bin or basket hidden away somewhere and pulled out for special occasions. Update it periodically when you're making other purchases at a wholesale, party or dollar store, or when you see fun accessories that would make for a great addition to your collection of balloons, streamers, party hats, confetti and other festive supplies.

BANNERS, BUNTING AND OTHER HANGING DECORATIONS

Widely available at party supply, craft and online stores, birthday banners and bunting are critical party decorations, and can be purchased to suit almost any theme. Place them in windows and doorways, string them up between trees, hang them along the side of a house or storage shed or display them pretty much anywhere there's space—on the mantle, above a bed, around a curtain rod or on any large, empty wall. Treat paper streamers the same way, using them to add a burst of colour to a large empty space. Twist and tie different colours together to create visual interest, or hang strips in a doorway to mimic a curtain—you can even cut the edges into a fringe for a different look altogether. Most hanging decorations can be strung up using removable tape, string, twine, nails or adhesive putty. Reusable cloth banners are also available for purchase, and while they are more of an investment, they can be used for years and years to come and passed down to children for use with their own families some day.

BALLOONS

These blown-up bundles of fun are an essential embellishment to almost any party, and the easiest way to make a room instantly feel festive. Abundance is key here, and the more balloons you can cluster together, the better; so don't hold back when adding balloons to a room or decorating a guest of honour's chair. Balloons can be found at most grocery, dollar, discount and party stores, and by keeping a collection of assorted colours, shapes and sizes readily available, you'll be ready to decorate almost any space with flair.

CANDLES

Available in a variety of shapes, colours and sizes, birthday candles are a crucial adornment on any celebration confection. Choose your candles carefully, basing them on the size of the cake and the person blowing them out. Classic birthday cakes look lovely when topped with long, skinny candles, while small, one-layer cakes look best with shorter options, like number or letter candles. To make a statement, use sparklers, which never fail to delight kids of all ages. Just make sure the birthday boy or girl doesn't mind that they can't blow them out.

Crepe and tissue paper can easily be transformed into simply statement-making party decorations with a small amount of time and effort. Perhaps the most popular way to use tissue paper is to make poufy pompoms that you can hang from ceilings, doorways and trees. Crepe paper can be used in place of streamers and strung up around a space for added colour and a touch of pizzazz. A roll of butcher paper is a good thing to have hanging around and can easily double as a disposable table covering, giant party sign or last-minute gift wrap. Lastly, keep some paper confetti in assorted sizes on hand and use it to cover tables or give to the kids to toss at the guest of honour. It's colourful and adds instant fun to a party.

CAKE DECORATING ACCESSORIES

Birthday cake is almost always the highlight of any child's party, and when liberally smeared with sticky icing and vibrant decorations it's easily the focus of much attention and adoration. Making these celebration confections can be as easy or as complicated as the baker desires, but keeping a few specific tools in your party closet will help make the job a straightforward task, regardless of skill:

- assorted cake pans: 6-inch (15 cm), 8-inch (20 cm), 9-inch (23 cm), 10-inch (25 cm) and a half-sheet pan
- palate knife: small, medium and large
- off-set spatula: one small
- piping bags, tips (round, star, leaf) and a coupler
- parchment paper
- assorted gel-paste food colourings
- cake stands
- rotating cake stand (optional)

BIG BIRTHDAY CAKE SANDWICH

This fun twist on a traditional deli sandwich is based on the Swedish specialty known as smörgåstårta, a savoury stack of mixed breads and assorted fillings that usually includes copious amount of mayonnaise, egg and cream cheese. This version is more kid-friendly, and definitely less messy, and can be made to suit the tastes of any birthday boy or girl.

¼ cup (60 mL) mayonnaise

½ cup (125 mL) Dijon mustard

1 large round loaf of bread

iceberg, Boston or butter lettuce

assorted deli meats like black forest ham, salami, roast beef and smoked turkey

assorted cheeses, thinly sliced

1 carrot, peeled and sliced into ribbons

birthday candles

- In a small bowl, combine the mayonnaise and mustard and set aside.

- Using a serrated knife, level the top of the loaf of bread by removing the fop slice of the dome. Cut the remaining loaf horizontally into four layers and brush all but the top piece with the mayonnaise-Dijon spread. Top each section with lettuce, meat and cheese, arranging the combinations however you like.

- Place the bottom layer of bread on a cake plate and top with a second piece of bread. Place the third layer on and top with the final, undressed piece of bread.

- Decorate the top of the "cake" with carrot ribbons and candles. To serve, cut the sandwich into wedges like a cake.

Serves 8–10

MINI BIRTHDAY CAKE SANDWICH

This celebratory sandwich is a piece of cake to put together, and can easily be served to a crowd of kids by multiplying the recipe as many times as required to feed the number of guests in attendance.

4 slices sandwich bread

sandwich spreads, like peanut butter, jam, cream cheese, chocolate-hazelnut spread, etc.

rainbow sprinkles

graduated cookie cutters, in various sizes

birthday candles

- Using the bread and sandwich filling(s) of choice, assemble 2 sandwiches.
- Take the largest cookie cutter and cut a shape from one of the sandwiches. Using the medium and small-sized cookie cutters, cut shapes from the centre of the second sandwich.
- Stack the cut pieces on a plate or platter in order from largest to smallest and scatter sprinkles over the top of the "cake". Insert a candle into the centre of the top tier and light it just before serving.

PARTY POINTER Ensure none of your guests are allergic to nuts before using nut butters in your sandwich fillings.

Makes 1 sandwich

BROWN RICE CRISP TREATS

This healthier alternative to traditional rice crisp treats is fairly forgiving, so feel free to experiment with other nut butters if you like.

1 Tbsp (15 mL) canola oil

⅔ cup (160 mL) natural peanut or almond butter

⅔ cup (160 mL) brown rice syrup or honey

1 tsp (5 mL) vanilla

6 cups (1.5 L) brown rice cereal

- Grease the inside of an 8 × 8-inch (20 × 20 cm) square baking pan with the oil and set aside.

- In a medium saucepan set over medium heat combine the peanut butter, brown rice syrup and vanilla and heat until thick and syrupy, about 2 minutes.

- Place the cereal in a large bowl and pour the syrup mixture over it, mixing thoroughly. Press the cereal into the prepared pan with the back of a rubber spatula or spoon. Transfer to the fridge and refrigerate for 1 hour. Cut into squares or rectangles with a sharp knife. Store in the fridge for up to 2 days.

Makes 9 large or 16 small treats

FINGER SANDWICHES

Simple sandwiches get a makeover in this elegant presentation of a classic party staple. From peanut butter and jam to hummus and veggies, a variety of favourite fillings can be used to make these traditional teatime snacks stand out.

whole-wheat sandwich bread

white sandwich bread

butter, softened

assorted fillings

square tray or platter

- Using 2 pieces of bread per sandwich, place slices on a work surface and cover half the pieces with a thick smear of butter. Top the same pieces with one of your sandwich fillings and then cover with the second piece of bread.

- To make traditional finger sandwiches, remove the crusts from the sandwiches and cut each sandwich into 4 triangles or 4 rectangles. Repeat with the remaining sandwiches.

- To make square sandwiches, remove the crusts from each sandwich and cut the bread into quarters.

- To make spiral tea sandwiches, ask your bakery department to slice the sandwich bread horizontally, or Pullman style. Flatten slices slightly using a rolling pin, then cover with butter and spread toppings over top. Roll up tightly, wrap each individual roll in plastic wrap and refrigerate for a minimum of 2 hours. Using a serrated knife, cut the ends off of each sandwich roll, then slice into 6–8 pieces.

PARTY POINTER Stacking the sandwiches and using an electric knife to cut through multiple pieces of bread at one time allows you to work twice as quickly. For variety, make 2 (or even 3) different fillings for the sandwiches.

Makes as many as needed

12 KID-APPROVED SANDWICH FILLING IDEAS

There's no doubt that kids love sandwiches. The following fillings are popular options for young eaters:

- peanut butter and Nutella
- bacon, lettuce and tomato
- apricot jam and Black Forest ham
- peanut butter and jam
- almond butter and honey
- cream cheese and cucumber
- cream cheese and strawberry jam
- tuna salad
- egg salad
- hummus and veggies
- ham, Brie and apple
- chicken salad

CRACKER-COATED CHICKEN STRIPS

I've been using this recipe for chicken strips ever since my teenager was a kindergartener, and it has endured through all sorts of situations with all types of kids. Choose crackers that are sturdy—saltines work well—and turn them into crumbs by pulsing in a food processor until a coarse crumb remains, or by placing them in a re-sealable bag and bashing with a rolling pin.

2 lb (1 kg) boneless skinless chicken breasts

1 cup (250 mL) plain yogurt

1 tsp (5 mL) kosher salt

½ tsp (2.5 mL) fresh ground pepper

1 Tbsp (15 mL) Dijon mustard

½ tsp (2.5 mL) Tabasco or other hot sauce

canola or other mild vegetable oil, for frying or baking

2 cups (500 mL) cracker crumbs

· Place the chicken breasts (one at a time) into a large re-sealable bag and pound the meat with a rolling pin until thickness is even throughout. Slice each chicken breast into 1-inch (2.5 cm) wide strips and set aside.

· Combine the yogurt, salt, pepper, mustard and hot sauce in a bowl; add the chicken and toss to combine. Cover with plastic wrap and place in the fridge for a minimum of 30 minutes or up to 1 day.

· When ready to cook the chicken, heat about half an inch of oil in a large, heavy skillet or preheat the oven to 400°F (200°C). Remove chicken from the yogurt marinade, shaking off any excess marinade, and dredge through the crackers, coating all sides well. Lay chicken pieces in the hot oil and cook, without crowding the pan, about 2 minutes per side or until golden brown and crispy. Transfer to a paper towel–lined plate.

· If baking, place the chicken pieces on a parchment-lined baking sheet and drizzle a small amount of oil over the strips. Bake for 15–20 minutes, turning the pieces over halfway through the cooking time, or until the chicken is thoroughly cooked and the crackers are golden brown; serve warm.

PARTY POINTER Chicken strips can be prepared up to one month in advance. Place marinated and coated chicken pieces on a parchment-lined baking sheet and freeze for 2–3 hours or until completely solid. Transfer the pieces to a re-sealable freezer bag, remove the excess air and freeze for up to 30 days. To bake, add an additional 5 minutes to the cooking time, if necessary.

Serves 6

DIY PASTA SALAD BAR

Kids will love the DIY component of this salad bar, and parents will love seeing something healthy and colourful on their childrens' plates. For younger kids, serve in small plastic bowls or paper cups for easy eating.

large bowl cooked rotini, bowtie or wagon wheel pasta, lightly tossed in oil to prevent pasta from sticking

small bowl cubed mozzarella cheese

small bowl cubed cheddar cheese

small bowl shaved Parmesan cheese

small bowl cherry tomatoes

small bowl diced cucumber

small bowl sliced green onions

small bowl sliced red bell pepper

small bowl sliced carrots

small bowl sliced pepperoni

small bowl chopped ham

small bowl shredded chicken

small bowl chopped basil leaves

small bowl croutons

assorted sauces: pesto, pizza sauce, olive oil and store-bought ranch dressing

• Lay the bowls out on a table in a line, and place the sauces at the end. Let guests customize their creations and have fun.

PARTY POINTER Create a list of customized combinations and print them to place at the salad bar for the kids to see. Examples include "Pizza Salad" made with pasta, pepperoni, mozzarella cheese, basil and pizza sauce, or "Cobb Salad" with pasta, tomatoes, cheddar cheese, ham, croutons and ranch dressing.

Serves as many as needed

BIRTHDAY PARTY POPCORN

You can successfully use microwave, stovetop or air-popped popcorn with this sweet treat and the end result will be the same. If you choose to use the microwavable kind, look for a natural or neutral variety, which will be less salty. If using stovetop or air-popped kernels, I encourage you to salt it lightly to offset the sweetness in the chocolate.

10 cups (2.5 L), or one 3.3 oz (100 g) pkg popped popcorn, lightly salted

2 cups (500 mL) crisp rice cereal

2 cups (500 mL) pretzels, crushed into small pieces

1 cup (250 mL) plain, peanut or mini M&Ms

10 oz (300 g) white chocolate, melted

5 Tbsp (75 mL) coloured sprinkles

- Combine the popcorn, cereal, pretzels and M&Ms in a large mixing bowl and dump onto a parchment lined baking sheet.

- Melt the white chocolate in the microwave in 20-second intervals, or by placing a heatproof bowl over a pot of simmering water. Drizzle the chocolate over the popcorn and, working swiftly, mix it into the popcorn mixture with a rubber spatula.

- Spread the popcorn evenly on the baking sheet, applying pressure with the spatula to create a nice uniform layer. Scatter the sprinkles over the popcorn before the chocolate hardens, to ensure they will stick. Set aside for 30–60 minutes or until the chocolate hardens. Break into pieces before serving.

Serves a medium-sized crowd

CANDY SUSHI PLATTER

Creating sushi look-alikes with candy is a cinch, and this colourful birthday party confection is certain to be popular with partygoers. This recipe makes two types of sushi, maki rolls and *nigiri*-style pieces with faux fish on top, but you can omit the instructions for one or the other and make all of your sushi identical, if desired.

rice crisp cereal squares, store-bought or homemade (page 91)

assorted candies including gummy fish, gummy worms, jelly beans, brightly coloured taffy, fruit leather, etc.

chopsticks

TO MAKE NIGIRI-STYLE SUSHI

- Slice regular-sized crisp rice squares into thin rectangles. Place a gummy fish or gummy worm on top, then wrap a thin piece of fruit leather around the base of the candy and over the fish, securing it in place by pressing the edges of the fruit leather together.

TO MAKE MAKI-STYLE SUSHI

- Flatten a rice square using a rolling pin. Lay it on top of a piece of fruit leather. Cut long, thin slices of red, orange and green taffy and lay them across the rice square lengthwise. Roll the candy up into a cylinder and slice into pieces.

TO MAKE PICKLED GINGER

- Cut a piece of orange taffy into thin slices and roll it out with a rolling pin. Starting with one end, wind the candy into a spiral, leaving a little space between each layer.

TO MAKE WASABI

- Slice green jelly beans in half and pile together.

Serve with chopsticks. Serves as many as needed.

ONE-BOWL CHOCOLATE BIRTHDAY CAKE

Baking this straightforward birthday confection is so easy it'll be tough to know who's more excited come the big day: you, for the ease with which you were able to assemble this home-made sweet, or the birthday boy or girl who has the honour of blowing out the candles that sit atop this gorgeous cake.

butter, for greasing the baking pans

1¾ cups (435 mL) all-purpose flour

¾ cup (185 mL) cocoa powder, plus extra for dusting

2 cups (500 mL) packed dark brown sugar

¾ tsp (4 mL) baking powder

2 tsp (10 mL) baking soda

1 tsp (5 mL) salt

1 cup (250 mL) buttermilk

½ cup (125 mL) vegetable oil

2 large eggs

1 Tbsp (15 mL) vanilla

1 cup (250 mL) boiling water (or hot coffee)

Fluffy Vanilla Frosting (page 105)

- Preheat the oven to 350°F (175°C). Butter two 8-inch (20 cm) round cake pans, line bottoms with parchment paper, and butter the paper. Dust the pans with cocoa, tapping out the extra.

- Combine the flour, cocoa powder, sugar, baking powder, baking soda and salt in a large bowl and stir well. Add the buttermilk, oil, eggs and vanilla and beat with a handheld or electric mixer for 2 minutes. Add the hot water to the cake batter, mixing well.

- Pour batter into pans, dividing it evenly. Bake for 30–35 minutes or until the centre is springy to the touch and a wooden toothpick or skewer inserted into the middle of the cake comes out clean. Cool completely before frosting.

- To assemble the cake, place one layer upside down on a cake plate or stand, then mound half of the fluffy vanilla frosting over top, spreading it evenly over the surface of the cake. Place the second layer on top, also upside down, and cover with the remaining frosting. The sides of the cake will not be iced. Decorate the top of the cake as desired, with colourful sprinkles or fresh fruit, and candles.

PARTY POINTER Cakes can be baked and frozen a few weeks in advance. Allow them to cool completely before wrapping each layer in a double layer of plastic wrap, followed by one layer of aluminum foil. To keep them from losing their shape or becoming squashed, place each layer on a cardboard round and stack them carefully inside the freezer. Frozen cakes are also easier to ice, as the crumbs don't stray into the icing as it's being spread over the cake. Another added benefit to freezing is that the process locks in moisture ensuring your cake doesn't end up dry.

Serves 8–10

HOW TO MAKE A QUICK BUTTERMILK SUBSTITUTE

Buttermilk adds tenderness to cake crumbs and lightens batter. If you don't have buttermilk in the fridge you can make a similar substitute by combining:

- 1 scant cup (approximately 240 mL) whole milk
- 1 Tbsp (15 mL) lemon juice or white vinegar

Combine the milk and lemon juice (or white vinegar) and let stand for 5–10 minutes, without stirring. Once ready, the milk will be slightly thickened with small curdled bits at the bottom. Stir well and use in your recipe where buttermilk is required.

FLUFFY VANILLA FROSTING

Commonly known as ermine or boiled milk frosting, this not-too-sweet fluffy vanilla icing is ideal for birthday cakes of all kinds. Similar in texture to a Swiss meringue buttercream, this milk and flour version provides the same smooth texture and creamy taste, but without the heavy butter flavour. It's important to note that while you may be tempted to make this frosting with a skim or lower fat milk, I wouldn't suggest it. However, if your family drinks a lighter milk and you don't want to purchase whole milk just for the purpose of making this icing, feel free to combine ½ cup (125 mL) reduced fat milk and ½ cup (125 mL) whipping cream; this combination works perfectly every time. Note: This recipe only makes enough icing to cover the tops of the two layers. It does not yield the quantity required to ice a cake in its entirety. You can successfully double the icing recipe should you wish to frost the whole cake, sides included.

¼ cup (60 mL) all-purpose flour

1 cup (250 mL) whole milk

1 cup (250 mL) butter, at room temperature

1 tsp (5 mL) vanilla

2 cups (500 mL) icing sugar, sifted

- Place a small saucepan over medium-low heat and whisk together the flour and milk. Continue cooking, while whisking constantly, until completely smooth and lump-free and until the thickness resembles pudding. Remove from the heat and scrape into a bowl.

- Let cool for 1 minute, then cover with a piece of plastic wrap, pressing it down onto the surface of the mixture in order to prevent a layer of skin from forming. Cool completely at room temperature— this can take anywhere from 1–3 hours.

- Using a handheld or electric mixer, cream the butter and vanilla. Add the icing sugar and beat on high for 3–4 minutes, or until light and airy; add the milk and flour mixture and continue beating until very fluffy. This could take several minutes, and at first it might seem as though the frosting is separating, but continue beating on high until it comes together and whips into a thick and smooth cloud-like consistency. Frost cake as per recipe directions.

Makes 3 cups (750 mL)

HOW TO DECORATE CAKES EASILY

There is no denying that the highlight of almost every birthday party is the cake, a celebration confection often covered in sweet frosting and edible decorations. Usually considered the visual centerpiece of a party, it's important for the cake to look festive and fabulous, and sometimes to display a theme, which can be a challenge for those who may not be confident in their cake decorating skills. The good news, though, is that there are many ways to adorn a cake with pretty accessories, even without actually knowing how to use a piping bag or other specialty baking tools.

For example, you can purchase small toys that are geared towards childrens' specific interests, or that express the theme of the party, and place them on top of the cake. Alternately, you can make adorable toppers by tying tiny balloons to wooden skewers and inserting them into the centre of the cake. Or blanket the sides of your cake in candy bar pieces, covering the top with mini cookies or other edible treats. It's even possible to make a banner or bunting with candy necklaces by cutting the string and tying the ends to two wooden skewers, neatly inserting them into the top of the cake.

For cupcakes, consider baking the batter in a flat-bottomed ice cream cone (this is especially great for birthdays that take place during warm-weather months) and cover the cone with a swirl of icing, a maraschino cherry and assorted sprinkles. Or, you can place a small numbered cookie cutter on top of an iced cupcake and fill the shape in with jimmies (long, thin, coloured sprinkles), highlighting the age of the birthday boy or girl. The options are endless, most are easy, and making cakes look pretty really isn't as difficult as it may seem.

BACKYARD *Barbecue*

SUMMER WEATHER IS a great excuse to dine al fresco, and it's usually easier to fit more people in the backyard than the dining room. If you don't have patio furniture, or what you have isn't enough to seat everyone, don't fret—people are generally happy to stand around in their flip-flops, nibbling on ribs. Or grab a few blankets to spread out on the grass and encourage kids and adults to get comfy and eat picnic-style. An outdoor barbecue is the ultimate in laid-back entertaining, all you need to do is mow your lawn and ensure you have enough fuel (or briquettes!) for the 'cue.—JVR

BACKYARD BEVVIES

A big tub or cooler of ice will keep drinks cold and accessible; beyond the usual wine, beer, Prosecco and pop or juice for the kids, consider making a big batch of lemonade or iced tea and dividing it into Mason jars. Putting lids on the jars means that you can sink them deep into the ice to keep them cold; all your guests need to do is unscrew the lids and they can drink straight from the jar. For something a little fancier, add fresh berries or a few fresh herbs (such as basil or thyme) to each jar before adding the lemonade. To make a basic lemonade concentrate, simmer equal parts lemon juice and sugar until the sugar dissolves; cool and chill, then add water—or sparkling water—to taste.

PLANKED BRIE

My friend Rockin' Ronnie Shewchuk, author of *Planking Secrets,* showed me how to plank a Brie—it's totally brilliant, and you can serve it straight from the smoldering plank (put something underneath if you're worried about the table!) with crackers or crusty bread. Top it with anything you might top a baked Brie with; just make sure you start with a food-grade plank—you can generally find them for a few dollars in the seafood section of the grocery store.

1 small wheel of Brie

½ cup (125 mL) fruit chutney or onion jam

1 cedar plank

- Soak your plank in the sink, weighted down with a pot or pan, for about 1 hour. Preheat your grill and place the plank on it for 5 minutes, or until it starts to smolder. Have a spray bottle of water at the ready to diffuse flare-ups.

- Cut a thin slice of rind off the top of the Brie and discard. Place the Brie on the plank and spoon the chutney or onion jam on top. Cook for 5–10 minutes, spraying any flames with water, until the cheese starts to melt—it will continue to melt as it sits on the warm plank.

- Serve immediately, with crackers or crusty bread.

Serves 6–8

FALL-OFF-THE-BONE RIBS

The trick to ultra-tender ribs is to precook them before they go on the barbecue; if they're only cooked on the grill, they'll wind up tough. Many people boil their ribs, but I find that process messy, and it simmers away so much of the meaty flavour. I find it easier to roast mine in the oven, covered with foil on a rimmed baking sheet; the roasted ribs can then be stashed in the fridge to finish on the grill whenever you're ready for them. Barbecue sauce is typically pretty sweet, and saving it for the end also keeps it from burning.

2 racks side or back pork ribs, trimmed of excess fat

¼–½ cup (60–125 mL) dry all-purpose barbecue rub, or salt and pepper

1 cup (250 mL) bottled barbecue sauce

- Preheat the oven to 300°F (150°C). Lay your pork ribs on a rimmed baking sheet and sprinkle generously with the dry rub (if you don't have a dry spice rub, a generous sprinkle of salt and pepper will do). Massage it into the meat, flipping over to coat the underside of the ribs as well as the top. Place them bone-down and cover tightly with foil.

- Bake for 2½ hours, until the meat is very tender. At this point, the ribs can be cooled, wrapped in foil and refrigerated for up to 3 days. When you're ready to grill, preheat your barbecue to medium-high, slather your ribs with sauce and grill for 15 minutes, turning as necessary and brushing with more sauce until the ribs are heated through and the exterior is dark, sticky and caramelized.

Serves 6

GRILLED BALSAMIC VEGGIES

A platter of charred veggies is a perfect side dish at any barbecue, and fresh zucchini, peppers, purple onions or whatever you bring home from the farmers' market can be cooked right on the grill, alongside anything else. I didn't use measurements here because you don't need them; simply douse any quantity of fresh veggies with oil and balsamic vinegar and you're good to go.

zucchini, cut lengthwise into ¼-inch (0.6 cm) strips

eggplant, cut lengthwise into ¼-inch (0.6 cm) strips

red, yellow or orange bell peppers, cored and quartered lengthwise

purple onions, cut into thin wedges

a few cloves of garlic, crushed

olive oil

balsamic vinegar

salt and pepper

· Put your prepared veggies in a shallow dish, add a few cloves of garlic and drizzle generously with olive oil and balsamic vinegar in about equal amounts. Let sit for at least 20 minutes, or cover and refrigerate for a few hours or overnight.

· Preheat the grill to medium-high and cook the veggies directly on the grill, turning with tongs until tender and charred in spots. If you like, drizzle with any oil and vinegar left over in the bottom of the marinating dish. Sprinkle with salt and pepper and serve.

Serves as many as needed

GRILLED ROMAINE CAESAR SALAD

Grilling your Caesar salad adds a wonderfully smoky flavour; it's a unique way of serving a summer classic.

DRESSING

½ cup (125 mL) canola or olive oil

2 garlic cloves, crushed

3 Tbsp (45 mL) mayonnaise

2 Tbsp (30 mL) lemon juice

1 Tbsp (15 mL) grainy or Dijon mustard

¼ cup (60 mL) freshly grated Parmesan cheese

freshly ground black pepper

SALAD

3 heads romaine lettuce

12 slices baguette

canola or olive oil, for cooking

freshly grated Parmesan cheese

- Trim the larger leaves from the outside of the heads of romaine and cut the heads in half lengthwise, leaving the stems intact. Start making the dressing: put the oil in a jar and add the garlic; shake or swirl around to combine. Brush both sides of the baguette slices with the garlicky oil and set aside on a plate.

- Add the remaining dressing ingredients to the jar and shake to combine. Preheat the grill to medium-high. Brush the cut side of the romaine with oil and place directly on the grill. Cook, turning as needed, until char-marked on both sides. Place the pieces of baguette on the grill as well and turn until toasted and char-marked. Leave them whole or transfer to a cutting board and roughly chop them.

- Place a grilled romaine on a serving platter (or one-half on each serving plate) and top with toasted baguette. Drizzle with dressing and scatter with extra Parmesan cheese. Serve immediately, while the lettuce is still warm.

Serves 6

GRILLED STRAWBERRY POUND CAKE

While the grill is hot, you might as well throw your dessert on there too. Firm slices of pine-apple, fresh mango cheeks and peach halves can be brushed with oil and cooked directly on the grill to serve with ice cream, but I like to go a step beyond and grill thick slabs of pound cake, with strawberries simmering in a foil packet alongside. It's like strawberry shortcake, without turning on the oven.

1 homemade or store-bought plain pound cake

1 lb (500 g) strawberries, hulled and halved

⅓ cup (80 mL) sugar, or to taste (divided)

1 cup (250 mL) heavy (whipping) cream

- Cut the pound cake into 1-inch (2.5 cm) thick slices. Place the strawberries on a double thickness of foil and sprinkle with about ¼ cup (60 mL) of the sugar, then bring up each side of foil and fold to enclose, crimping the edges to make a well-sealed package.

- Place the foil packet directly on the grill, in a cooler spot if possible. Grill the pound cake directly on the grill, turning with tongs until toasted and grill-marked. When the foil packet of berries is thoroughly hot, remove it and set aside to cool slightly.

- Meanwhile, beat the cream with the remaining sugar until soft peaks form. Carefully open the packet of strawberries and pour the juicy berries over each piece of grilled pound cake. Top with a dollop of whipped cream.

Serves 6

HOW TO HAVE A BLOCK PARTY

Every summer, our neighbours one block over close off their street and throw a party. They live in a cul-de-sac, which makes closing it off easy, and the guys at the end of the block are in a band, so they rent a stage and perform live music.

Elaborate or not, a street party is a great way to get to know the people you share your community with. Most block parties are big and bustling and casual, with neighbours spilling out onto the street to eat and chat and play. The tricky part is in the planning; here are a few things to consider:

- Block parties work best on streets that don't see a lot of traffic—you may not be able to get permission to block it off otherwise. Contact someone at city hall well in advance about what permits are needed.

- If closing off a block is impossible, consider organizing it where space permits in a nearby public park.

- Let your neighbours know weeks ahead of time what you're planning—print off flyers and put them into mailboxes, letting everyone know about the event (and hopefully enlisting volunteers to help). Start an online group so that all efforts can be coordinated in one place.

- Consider renting tents, a popcorn or cotton candy machine, a bouncy castle, sumo suits or other party games; your community association may have funds available to offset the cost of rentals.

- Ask teenagers to set up face painting or temporary tattoo stations, hand out balloons or organize a play area for younger kids.

- Pick up plenty of sidewalk chalk and draw hopscotch games on the street, then encourage kids to do their own decorating as a lasting reminder of the fun day you had.

- Make it a potluck and ask local businesses if they're willing to donate food or drinks, or roll a few barbecues from backyards into the street to grill up burgers and dogs.

- Since the street will be blocked off, encourage people to bring out tables and chairs, ride-on toys, scooters and tricycles and anything else that contributes to the fun.

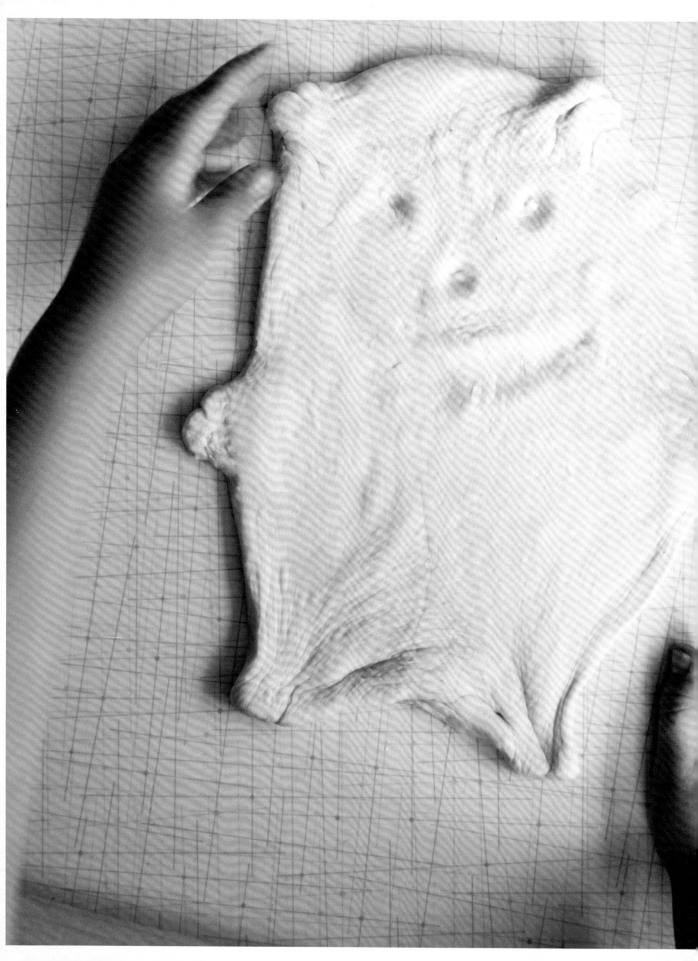

PIZZA *Party*

I KNOW PLENTY of families who declare Fridays "pizza night"—the idea of cozying down with a chewy, cheesy pizza at the end of a long week has huge appeal. If it's part of your weekend ritual, having a great recipe for homemade dough in your back pocket is invaluable, and if you need an easy way to feed a large group of people—particularly young ones—DIY pizza is the way to go. The presence of pizza itself is enough to make it a party.—JVR

GO-TO PIZZA DOUGH

Homemade pizza dough can be the starting point for any number of dishes, from straight-up pizza to calzone or even breadsticks. After a few batches, you'll be able to stir it up by memory.

1 cup (250 mL) lukewarm water

1 tsp (5 mL) sugar

2 tsp (10 mL) active dry yeast

2½–3 cups (625–750 mL) all-purpose flour

1 Tbsp (15 mL) extra virgin olive or canola oil

1 tsp (5 mL) salt

- Put the water in a large bowl and sprinkle the sugar and yeast over top; let stand for 5 minutes, until it's foamy.

- Add 2½ cups (625 mL) of the flour, the oil and salt and stir until the dough comes together. Using a dough hook on your stand mixer or on a lightly floured surface, knead the dough for about 8 minutes, adding more flour if the dough is too sticky. Work the dough until it's smooth and elastic, and slightly tacky.

- Place back in the bowl—if you like, drizzle it with oil and turn to coat the dough all over—then cover with a tea towel and let sit for 1 hour, until doubled in size. Punch it down and you're ready to use it.

- To make pizza, divide the dough into 2–3 pieces, and roll each as thin as you can, with a slightly higher edge. On a heavy baking sheet scattered with flour or cornmeal, spread the dough with tomato sauce, sprinkle with toppings and bake in a preheated 450°F (230°C) oven for 15–20 minutes, until bubbly and golden.

Makes enough for 2–3 pizzas

BEYOND PEPPERONI

Anything goes when it comes to pizza, but there are a few things to keep in mind. Meats should be cured (ham and pepperoni) or cooked (ground beef, chicken), and while most veggies can be added fresh, the juicy ones can release liquid as they cook, making your pizza soggy. Try sundried tomatoes and roasted red peppers instead of their fresh counterparts, and give spinach or chard, onions and mushrooms a quick sauté in olive oil—add garlic for one of the tastiest pizza toppings ever. Pesto or barbecue sauce can be used in place of traditional tomato sauce, and try crumbling feta, Boursin or goat cheese or laying thin slices of Brie or Cambozola in place of (or along with) grated or torn fresh mozzarella. Some of our favourite pizza combos:

- cooked ground lamb with garlic, Boursin and sautéed chard
- caramelized onions and Cambozola
- bacon, mushrooms and roasted red pepper
- leftover roasted or grilled veggies with crumbled feta

CHEWY, CHEESY BREADSTICKS

To make breadsticks, pull the pizza dough (see Go-To Pizza Dough, page 123) into chunks and roll into thin ropes; twist two ropes together and place on a parchment-lined sheet. Crush a clove of garlic into a small ramekin of oil and brush mixture over the breadsticks. Sprinkle breadsticks with freshly grated Parmesan cheese and bake at 350°F (175°C) for 15 minutes, until golden. Serve warm.

SAUSAGE, MUSHROOM AND SPINACH CALZONE

Calzones are fancy pizza pockets, made with pizza dough folded over to enclose the filling. They can be great for a kids' party, to pack for a camping trip (wrap them in foil and rewarm by the fire) or just for something a little different on pizza night.

canola or olive oil, for cooking

2–3 fresh Italian sausages

2–3 cups (500–750 mL) sliced mushrooms

2–3 cups (500–750 mL) fresh baby spinach

1 cup (250 mL) tomato or spaghetti sauce

1–2 cups (250–500 mL) grated mozzarella, or a couple balls of fresh mozzarella, torn

1 batch pizza dough

· In a large, heavy skillet, heat a drizzle of oil over medium-high heat and squeeze the sausages out of their casings and into the pan. Cook, breaking up with a spoon, until the meat is no longer pink. Add the mushrooms and cook for 4–5 minutes, until soft and starting to turn golden on the edges. Add the spinach and tomato sauce and cook for about 5 minutes, until the spinach wilts and the mixture thickens.

· Preheat the oven to 450°F (230°C). Divide the pizza dough into 4–6 pieces and roll out very thin; mound some filling in the middle of each circle and sprinkle with cheese. Fold the dough over to enclose, pinching the edges to seal, and place on a parchment-lined baking sheet. Cut a few slits in the top with a sharp knife.

· Bake for 15–20 minutes, until bubbly and golden.

Makes 4–6 calzones

COOKIE PIZZA

A giant cookie made with a sugar dough crust and topped with chocolate, marshmallows, fruit and nuts can be a fun dessert, especially if there are kids around. Have dough ready to go and enlist help adding the toppings or squeezing on white chocolate "cheese".

CRUST

⅓ cup (80 mL) butter, at room temperature

2 Tbsp (30 mL) canola oil

¾ cup (185 mL) sugar

1 large egg

2 tsp (10 mL) vanilla

1½ cups (375 mL) all-purpose flour

1 tsp (5 mL) baking powder

¼ tsp (1 mL) salt

TOPPINGS

a selection of mini marshmallows, chocolate chips, M&Ms or other coated chocolate candies, chopped nuts and chopped dried fruit

½ cup (125 mL) chopped white chocolate

· In a large bowl, beat the butter, oil and sugar with an electric mixer until pale and light; add the egg and vanilla and beat for 1 minute, until smooth and well blended.

· In a small bowl, stir together the flour, baking powder and salt. Add to the sugar mixture and stir by hand or beat on low speed just until you have a soft dough. Shape the dough into a disc, wrap in plastic and refrigerate for half an hour.

· When you're ready to bake, preheat the oven to 350°F (175°C). Press the dough into two 8-inch (20 cm) round cake pans or shape it free-form into a ¼-inch (6 mm) thick round on a parchment-lined baking sheet. Bake for 15 minutes, until very pale golden; scatter with mini marshmallows, chocolate chips, dried fruit and nuts, and return to the oven for 5–10 minutes, until the marshmallows are golden.

· Remove from heat and let cool on a wire rack. Put the white chocolate into a zip-lock bag, seal and place in a bowl of warm water. Knead occasionally until the chocolate has melted. Snip off one corner and squeeze the chocolate out, drizzling over the pizzas to create a melted cheese effect.

· Cut into wedges to serve.

Makes about 1½ dozen wedges

HOW TO HOST A DIY PIZZA PARTY

A make-your-own-pizza party is ideal for any number of occasions—
birthday parties especially, since kids tend to be pizza enthusiasts and
making their own gives them something to do. But pizza is just as
appealing to adults—and because it cooks quickly, you can let friends
assemble their own to bake and eat, even with only one oven. DIY allows
each person to consider their own tastes—and dietary needs—and the
interactive element is a great ice breaker. It's fun to get everyone in the
kitchen (they'll be there anyway) and let loose on bowls of toppings and
grated cheese. Have a few in the oven as guests arrive, then set out balls
of dough, dishes of sauce, chopped or sautéed toppings and cheeses along
with a roll of parchment paper, so that each pizza can be assembled on
a piece of parchment and then easily slid onto a sheet for baking. Use
wooden boards for baked pizzas that are ready to be sliced, freeing up
each sheet as it comes out of the oven. Guests can eat their own or put
them out to share—and with a good stash of homemade dough at the
ready, you can crank out pizzas until everyone's full, with minimal effort
on your part.

SNOW Day

BEFORE I MET and married my husband, I lived in the South of France for a year. I was 21 years old, and with the exception of a weeklong vacation to Florida during high school, my previous travel experience had been limited to a few touristy destinations across the country.

I arrived in Nice on a crisp January morning, and as I walked through the sun soaked baggage claim looking for a French man with a black Chihuahua—the only identifying trait I had for the person who was going to employ me for the next year—I knew I was in for a wild ride. The dapper middle-aged man arrived two minutes after I did, and I spent the bulk of that year taking care of his two young sons and befriending his kind in-laws, who didn't speak a word of English, yet somehow successfully taught me to drive a stick shift. I also learned a lot about entertaining with efficiency and simplicity from the man's wife, a cool-tempered lady who was well acquainted with members of a royal family, played tennis and golf with the wealthy elite, and who came home to cook dinner for her husband and eight of his business associates with ease and elegance.

The family I was living with made their home in Monte Carlo, Monaco, a small principality along the Mediterranean Sea. Nestled nicely between France and Italy, it is best known for its swanky casinos, tax-free living and Grace Kelly. But to me, it was the place where I learned the most about purchasing produce at an outdoor market, making seductive soups from scratch, and simple, fuss-free in-home entertaining. Of all the lessons gleaned from my time there, the one that's most firmly planted in my memory is this: when the lady of the house entertains she never makes her main course the same day she plans on serving it. To this day, that golden nugget of wisdom has proven incredibly valuable, time and time again. It's how I approach any dish I plan on serving to guests, especially during the cold weather months when braises and bakes serve as ideal make-ahead meals intended for feeding a crowd.

Now that you know my secret for feeding many mouths in the dead of a cold and dreary winter, I encourage you to host your own snow day gathering. Invite a few of your favourite people to go sledding, skiing, skating, or to play a game of good old-fashioned shinny on an outdoor rink. Bundle the kids up and shuffle them outdoors to build snowmen and icy forts in the backyard, then call them back inside and serve them (and their parents!) steaming pots of baked chili spiked with sweet chocolate chips, or a beef stew that simmers in a bath of ale (and onions and is delightful when served with extra mustard and crunchy cornichons), or possibly even a simple slow-cooker chicken chili with all the fixings. Whatever you decide to do, don't let the cold weather prevent your from feasting with friends; it really is as easy as it seems.—JS

GATHERING IS GOOD FOR YOUR HEALTH

According to a 2010 study conducted by the scientific journal *PLOS Medicine* on social relationships and mortality risks, gathering with friends is good for your health. The degree of risk associated with a lack of social relationships (think dinners with friends, book clubs, parties, movie nights, coffee dates and getaways) is comparable to other well-established risk factors like smoking and obesity. In other words, eat, drink (moderately) and be merry with your friends as often as possible—your health depends on it!

BEEF IN BEER STEW

We are a winter family, through and through. While some folks prefer the sun, surf and sand that comes with summer, we're much more likely to spend time outdoors in the snow, frolicking in the frosty weather. And after a few hours playing hockey on the local rink, or tobogganing down a nearby hill, there's nothing better than the rich aroma of beef stewing in beer, greeting us at the front door as we stamp the snow from our books. I like to serve this dish with buttered egg noodles, but boiled or mashed potatoes pair just as well.

3½ lb (3.75 kg) boneless blade roast, excess fat trimmed, cut into 1-inch (2.5 cm) pieces

salt and pepper

¼ cup (60 mL) all-purpose flour

2 Tbsp (30 mL) olive oil

3 Tbsp (45 mL) butter

3 medium yellow onions, thinly sliced lengthwise

2 cups (500 mL) Belgian beer (like Chimay), or other dark ale

1 can condensed beef broth

1 bay leaf

3 thyme sprigs

3 carrots, peeled and sliced into ½-inch (1.3 cm) thick coins

2 Tbsp (30 mL) grainy Dijon mustard

2 Tbsp (30 mL) dark brown sugar

- Pat the beef dry with paper towels. Transfer to a large mixing bowl and generously season with salt and pepper; add the flour and toss to coat.

- Heat 1 Tbsp (15 mL) olive oil and the butter in a large Dutch oven set over medium-high heat. When the oil is simmering, brown the beef in batches, cooking each side for 2–3 minutes or until golden brown. Transfer to a plate and set aside.

- Preheat the oven to 300°F (150°C). When the beef has been browned, add the onions to the pot as well as the remaining 1 Tbsp (15 mL) of oil. Reduce heat to medium and cook until the onions are soft and caramelized, 15–20 minutes. Add 1 cup (250 mL) of beer and cook, scraping the browned bits from the bottom of the pot, until reduced by half.

- Return the beef and juices that have collected on a plate to the pot and add the remaining beer, beef broth, bay leaf, thyme, carrots, mustard and brown sugar. Bring to a boil, cover and transfer to the preheated oven. Cook for 2½ hours.

- Remove the stew from the oven and skim the excess fat from the sauce; discard the bay leaf and thyme sprigs. Check seasonings and adjust, if required.

PARTY POINTER This stew tastes even better when made in advance, so go ahead and prep it up to two days in advance of serving.

Serves 6

CHOCOLATE CHIP AND STOUT CHILI

This recipe comes from my friend Aimée, who originally sourced it from Nigella Lawson. In my version, the flavours are mild, keeping it very family friendly, but you can certainly boost the heat by adding a fresh sliced and seeded chile pepper, as Nigella suggests in her original recipe. You can serve this as part of a casual Mexican-inspired buffet by adding baskets of crisp tortilla chips, sour cream, shredded cheese, fresh cilantro, pickled jalapeños, green onions and lime wedges, or just as it is alongside a floury dinner roll or hunk of cornbread.

2 Tbsp (30 mL) olive oil

2 lb (1 kg) lean ground beef

2 lb (1 kg) sausages, casings removed

3 medium onions, peeled and finely chopped

4 cloves garlic, peeled and finely chopped

2 tsp (10 mL) ground cumin

1 tsp (5 mL) ground coriander

1 tsp (5 mL) ground cinnamon

½ tsp (2.5 mL) ground cardamom

2 Tbsp (30 mL) chili powder

one 5½ oz (156 mL) can tomato paste

¼ cup (60 mL) ketchup

three 14 oz (398 mL) cans red kidney beans, drained

three 14 oz (398 mL) cans crushed or diced tomatoes

one 16 oz (475 mL) can stout beer (such as Guinness)

½ cup (125 mL) semi-sweet chocolate chips

salt and pepper to taste

- Preheat the oven to 300°F (150°C). Heat the olive oil in a large oven-proof pot (with lid) and add the ground beef and sausage. Brown the meat on medium heat, breaking it up as it cooks.

- Add the onion and garlic and cook for until soft and translucent, about 8–10 minutes. Stir in the cumin, coriander, cinnamon, cardamom and chili powder; mix well to combine.

- Stir in the tomato paste, ketchup, beans and crushed tomatoes; add the stout and bring the chili to a boil.

- Once it starts bubbling, remove the pot from the heat. Sprinkle the chocolate chips over the chili, cover with the lid and transfer the pot to the oven, cooking for 3 hours. Check seasonings, adding salt and pepper if necessary. Serve hot.

PARTY POINTER This dish freezes beautifully and can be made a month or two in advance of serving. To reheat, allow the chili to defrost in the fridge, then transfer it to a pot and bring it to a boil over medium heat before serving.

Serves 8–10

SIMPLE SLOW-COOKER CHICKEN CHILI

This is one of those meals that can almost always be thrown together using just everyday items from a well-stocked pantry. It's simple enough to serve as a casual weeknight family dinner, but flavourful enough to offer to guests when you're entertaining on the weekend. It also works well as a sympathy meal: a comforting dish to take to friends and neighbours in need, or to new parents who are trying to make it through the chaotic days after a new arrival.

1 medium onion, diced

2 lb (1 kg) boneless, skinless chicken breast or thighs, cut into ½-inch (1 cm) pieces

2 Tbsp (30 mL) lime juice

1 tsp (5 mL) ground cumin

1 Tbsp (15 mL) chili powder

1 tsp (5 mL) dried oregano

pinch of cayenne (optional)

½ tsp (2.5 mL) each: kosher salt and fresh ground pepper

one 19 oz (540 mL) can pinto beans, drained and rinsed

two 19 oz (540 mL) cans navy beans, drained, rinsed and slightly mashed

2 cups (500 mL) salsa

1 cup (250 mL) chicken stock

- Combine all of the ingredients in a slow cooker and cook on low for 6 hours. Serve with nacho chips, sour cream, grated cheese, lime wedges and fresh cilantro, if desired.

PARTY POINTER This is a great dish to serve for Super Bowl Sunday or Hockey Night in Canada, along with cold beer and crisp nacho chips.

Serves 6

MAPLE APPLE UPSIDE-DOWN BUTTERMILK CAKE

Warm, soft apples coated in a thick maple sauce sit atop a basic buttermilk cake in a rustic winter sweet that's simple to prepare, yet pleases the palate in ways that will convince your guests you spent hours working on this dish. Feel free to use pears in place of the apples, and don't hesitate to drizzle a little extra maple syrup over the cold ice cream just before serving.

TOPPING

⅓ cup (80 mL) brown sugar

2 Tbsp (30 mL) butter, plus extra for pan

2 Tbsp (30 mL) pure maple syrup

2 Granny Smith apples, peeled and cored and cut into ¼-inch (0.6 cm) thick slices

CAKE

¼ cup (60 mL) butter, softened

¾ cup (185 mL) sugar

1 large egg

1 tsp (5 mL) vanilla

1 cup (250 mL) all-purpose flour

½ tsp (2.5 mL) baking powder

½ tsp (2.5 mL) baking soda

¼ tsp (1 mL) salt

½ cup (125 mL) buttermilk

vanilla ice cream, for serving

- Preheat oven to 350°F (175°C). Lightly butter an 8-inch (20 cm) round cake pan and place the brown sugar, butter and maple syrup in it. Place it into the oven as it preheats, removing when the butter is melted, then stir with a fork until smooth. Arrange the apples in two concentric circles, overlapping them slightly. Set aside.

- To make the cake, beat the butter and sugar in a large bowl until pale and fluffy, about 1–2 minutes. Mix in the egg and vanilla and beat for another 2 minutes. In a small bowl, stir together the flour, baking powder, baking soda and salt.

- By hand, or with a hand-held or electric mixer on low speed, add the flour mixture in 3 batches, alternating with buttermilk, beginning and ending with flour, and mixing just enough after each addition combine the ingredients. Dump the batter into the cake pan, over the apples, smoothing the top with a spatula.

- Bake for 35–40 minutes or until the cake is golden and spongy to the touch; let cool for 10 minutes, then invert onto a plate. Serve with whipped cream or vanilla ice cream, if desired.

PARTY POINTER This cake travels well and makes an excellent addition to any winter potluck or ski day outing.

Serves 8

WARM SPICED LEMONADE

This quintessential summer classic is also ideal for winter when it's warmed and infused with fragrant spices like ginger and cinnamon. Meyer lemons are in season and readily available during the winter months, so if you can find them we encourage you to use them in this recipe.

1 cup (250 mL) lemon juice (from 5–6 large lemons)

¾–1 cup (185–250 mL) sugar

4 cups (1 L) water

¼ cup (60 mL) fresh ginger, peeled and sliced (optional)

cinnamon sticks and lemon slices, for garnish

· Combine the water, ¾ cup (185 mL) of the sugar and ginger (if using) in a medium saucepan and bring to a boil. Simmer for 10 minutes; discard the ginger. Stir in lemon juice, heat through and taste. Add the remainder of the sugar, if desired. Ladle into mugs and serve with lemon slices and a cinnamon stick.

Serves 6

CASUAL WEEKNIGHT *Get-Together*

MOST OF US HAVE gatherings around the dinner table more often than we realize, and yet so often we overlook weeknights as opportunities to have people over. On a Wednesday a few years ago, a friend (who was married with two kids) sent an email from her office: "Hey, want to come over for chicken burgers tonight?" She picked up buns and bagged salad on the way home, we brought dessert, and it was a completely awesome way to spend an otherwise ordinary workday evening (because it's not what's on the table that matters, it's who's around it.)

The key here is ease. Weeknights tend to be more time-crunched, but we all have to eat anyway, so just think of it as a few more mouths to feed at dinner. Braised chicken in milk takes minutes to throw into a pot and slide into the oven, and the result is an unbelievably tender chicken that can be plunked directly on the table, right in the pot, for friends to dig into. Likewise, grainy lentil and hardy kale salads can be made in advance and stashed in the fridge, and brownie batter can be stirred together in five minutes to bake while everyone's eating.—JVR

LEMON-BRAISED CHICKEN IN MILK

Jamie Oliver taught me (indirectly, of course) to braise a whole chicken in milk. It is perhaps the easiest, tastiest chicken you'll ever eat, with hardly any preparation—and no basting—required. Throw a handful of herbs into the pot if you have some. It's also just as easy to do two chickens as it is to cook one, depending on how many you're expecting at the table—you'll just need a bigger pot.

1 whole chicken

salt and freshly ground black pepper

canola oil or butter, for cooking

1 lemon

1 head garlic, halved crosswise

2 cups (500 mL) thin-skinned new potatoes, halved (optional)

2 cups (500 mL) milk

· Preheat the oven to 375°F (190°C). Pat the chicken dry, season it with salt and pepper, and heat a heavy, ovenproof pot on the stovetop over medium-high heat. Add a drizzle of oil and brown the chicken all over, turning it with tongs.

· Add the remaining ingredients to the pot, cover and bake for 1½ hours, removing the lid for the last half an hour if you like to brown the top a little more.

· To serve, pull the meat off the bones and drizzle with sauce and a few soft cloves of the roasted garlic.

Serves 4–6

LENTIL AND BULGUR
SALAD WITH SPINACH AND FETA

A hearty, grainy salad made with lentils makes an easy side for roast chicken. It can be made the night before (or morning of) and stashed in the fridge until you're ready to eat.

1½ cups (375 mL) dry green, brown or du Puy lentils

extra virgin olive oil

balsamic vinegar

salt and pepper

2 cups (500 mL) chopped or torn baby spinach

½ cup (125 mL) dry bulgur or couscous

1 cup (250 mL) cherry or grape tomatoes, halved

½ cup (125 mL) crumbled feta or goat cheese

- Bring a medium saucepan of water to a boil. Add the lentils and cook for 30–40 minutes, until tender. Drain well in a colander and transfer to a bowl. While still hot, toss with oil and vinegar and season with salt and pepper to taste. If you like, add the spinach while the lentils are still warm, so that it wilts slightly.

- Meanwhile, place the bulgur in a bowl and cover with 1 cup (250 mL) of boiling water. Cover with a plate and let sit for 20 minutes, or until the bulgur has absorbed all the water. Drain any excess and add the bulgur to the lentil mixture; toss to combine and add more oil and vinegar, if necessary.

- Add tomatoes and feta (and the spinach, if you didn't add it earlier) and toss to combine.

Serves 6–8

LEMONY KALE AND BRUSSELS SPROUT SALAD

For a while, I was hopelessly addicted to this salad. I adapted it from one I found in *Bon Appétit*, and there was a period when we were eating it weekly, sometimes daily. It's a great recipe to feed a crowd, since a bunch of kale expands to many times its original bulk when thinly sliced. And it keeps well; the dressing acts as a marinade for the kale and Brussels sprouts, so you can toss it early and let it sit. (I'd hold the almonds back until serving time so that they keep their crunch.) Leftovers are fab topped with a fried egg.

1 small bunch kale

5-6 big Brussels sprouts

1 tart apple or ripe pear, chopped

¼-½ cup (60-125 mL) roasted, salted almonds, roughly chopped

½ cup (125 mL) freshly grated Parmesan or Pecorino

DRESSING

½ cup (125 mL) olive oil

¼ cup (60 mL) lemon juice

2 Tbsp (30 mL) grainy mustard

1 small garlic clove, finely grated

2 tsp (10 mL) honey

salt and freshly ground black pepper

- Hold each leaf of kale by its stem and pull off the leaves; stack and thinly slice the leaves (discard the stems), and put it all into a salad bowl. Halve the Brussels sprouts lengthwise and thinly slice them too, discarding the stems. Add to the bowl of kale, and add the apple (or pear).

- To make the dressing, shake all the ingredients together in a jar or whisk them in a small bowl. Drizzle generously over the kale, Brussels sprouts and apples and toss to coat.

- Scatter with almonds and Parmesan and serve, or refrigerate until you're ready for it.

Serves 6

BROWNED BUTTER BROWNIES

Katherine Hepburn's famous brownie recipe is almost the same as my Grandma's. It can be stirred together in minutes using only one pot, and go into the oven as you eat dinner. If you add a few extra minutes and brown the butter first, the result is even more divine. They're my go-to dessert when I need something quick that I know everyone will love.

½ cup (125 mL) butter

2 oz (2 squares) unsweetened chocolate

1 cup (250 mL) sugar

2 large eggs

1 tsp (5 mL) vanilla

¼ cup (60 mL) all-purpose flour

¼ tsp (1 mL) salt

- Preheat the oven to 350°F (175°C).

- In a medium saucepan, melt the butter and chocolate over medium heat. (If you like, heat the butter alone first, swirling the pan until it turns brown and nutty-smelling before adding the chocolate.) Remove from the heat and let sit a few minutes to cool slightly, and then stir in the sugar, eggs and vanilla.

- Add the flour and salt and stir just until combined. Line an 8 × 8-inch (20 × 20 cm) pan with parchment, letting the edges overhang, and spread the batter into the pan.

- Bake for 25–30 minutes, until the edges start to pull from the sides of the pan.

- Lift the brownie out using the edges of the parchment as handles, and cut into squares.

PARTY POINTER Serve the warm brownies straight from their parchment paper, or scoop them up warm into a bowl and top with a scoop of vanilla (or salted caramel!) ice cream and a drizzle of chocolate sauce.

Makes 16 brownies

HOW TO BE A GRACIOUS POTLUCK GUEST

- Show up on time. This is especially important if you are in charge of the appetizers/snacks or beverages. If you're running late, notify the host as soon as possible, but do everything you can to arrive at the time you are expected.

- Stick to the plan and don't change your mind about what you're bringing to the party unless ok'd to do so by the host.

- Have your dish ready as per the instructions of the host. If your recipe requires last-minute specialty equipment, counter space or the use of the stove, communicate this to the host before committing to your contribution.

- Wash and take care of your own dishes after the meal. Better yet, pack them up dirty and deal with them when you return home.

HOW TO HOST A POTLUCK

The term potluck has an old-fashioned ring to it, and immediately brings to mind cheerful bonnets, children dressed in their Sunday best and large covered dishes filled with jellied salads and tuna noodle casserole. In reality, a potluck gathering is an ideal way for the modern host to entertain, and lends itself well to everything from a casual weeknight dinner to a large holiday meal.

The very best potlucks are fun and relaxing, with a breezy tone that leaves everyone feeling comfortable. The key to success lies in the organization, and while there are a few guidelines to follow when planning (or attending) a potluck, there is only one traditional rule that should always be followed: each person brings a dish that is large enough to be shared among a good percentage, but not necessarily all, of the expected guests. For example, for a crowd of 20, each dish only needs to feed 10–12 people, not the entire group.

If you are hosting a potluck, the job of organizing is your responsibility. By definition alone, it's quite possible that this type of party could yield a random assortment of dishes that don't work well together at the table. In addition, without a plan in place, it's entirely feasible that you'll end up with three trays of lasagna. Therefore, the easiest way to organize who will bring what is to break down the meal into categories of contribution and go from there. I like to divide my dinner as follows:

- appetizers/snacks
- main dishes
- salads and sides
- desserts
- beverages

Decide what you, the host, will provide (it's usually the main course), then ask your guests what they would like to bring, giving them a choice between two of the remaining categories. This allows them to take their time and budget into consideration when making a decision. Keep track of the replies and fill in any gaps in the meal after your friends have committed to a dish.

The ultimate point of a potluck is to avoid putting excess stress or expense on the person hosting. It's also an excellent opportunity for guests to share their favourite dishes and recipes with others, which is reason alone to consider this style of gathering. Hosting is fun, but being cooked for is even more special, and a potluck party offers the benefits of both.

"To be a truly successful potluck host, here are some other things you'll want to keep in mind:"

- If guests are unsure of what to bring, don't hesitate to delegate specific dishes or recipes, or offer suggestions based on what others are preparing for the dinner.

- Dig out extra platters, baskets, napkins and serving utensils so that you have them readily available if they are required.

- Ask guests to fully prepare all dishes in advance of arriving.

- Request that foods come in easily transportable containers. For anything that calls for warming, specify that it arrive in a heatproof and/or microwave-safe dish.

- Let non-cooks know that it's okay to bring something store-bought if they are more comfortable with that option.

- Always compliment dishes that have been cooked by your guests and thank them for contributing to the meal.

- Ask for any known food allergies/intolerances in advance and ensure that the entire group is aware of them.

- Proper potluck etiquette dictates that leftovers should be left behind for the host or hostess. I think this is a mighty fine idea, but I also like the idea of divvying them up among guests, sending a little leftover goodness from the gathering home with everyone. Either option is fine, of course, but if you decide to send anything extra home with your friends, ask them to bring a clean re-sealable container to the dinner just in case they're lucky enough to take home the edible remains of the party.

HOLIDAY *Open House*

THE SECRET TO being a guest at your own party is to host an open house. Comprised of a low-maintenance, make-ahead menu, the food is served buffet-style and requires nothing more from a host than some rotational reheating of hot foods, and rapid replenishing of those that can be eaten cold or at room temperature.

An ideal time to open your home to friends and family is during the holidays, when the desire to host is the strongest, but you have the least amount of time to do it in. The tone for this type of gathering should be warm and casual—an open house offers a break to your prospective guests who are likely overwhelmed and over-committed by the season's schedule. It keeps the focus on the people in attendance and not the preparation, which naturally forces you to make merry with those you love. While a successful open house does require a small amount of strategic planning, in the end you're left with a party that works itself, leaving you free to roam the room and chat with your guests, which is the reason you've chosen to throw a party, anyways. I like to set up three easily accessible stations for my guests: a main buffet to hold the bulk of the food, a self-serve beverage bar, and a designated space for coffee and dessert. Even if you live in a small space, you can organize your party this way by making use of existing counter space, coffee and dining tables, sideboards and bookshelves; just clear our a row of books and use the space as your "bar", outfitting it with glasses, bottles and a bucket of ice (see How to Entertain in a Small Space, page 187).

For the menu, foods like glazed ham and spicy olives work well because they taste just as good for the first partygoers as the do for the last person who arrives. Round out the sweet treats with party pretzel sticks that can be prepared days in advance, and my Aunt's peanut butter balls with walnuts and dates, a treat that tastes just like Christmas to anyone in my family.

Lastly, don't forget to include a little ambiance in your open house planning. The first guests to arrive should feel as though the party is in full swing when you greet them at the door. Have your carefully selected tunes shuffling sounds through the house, candles and twinkle lights setting the place aglow, and scents wafting from the kitchen, even if it's just a pot of homemade air freshener bubbling on the stovetop.—JS

HOSTING A SUCCESSFUL OPEN HOUSE

- Avoid cooking during an open house; with guests coming and going at different times you want to be free from the kitchen so you can greet them appropriately.

- This should be the easiest type of gathering you host; keep self-serve in mind when it comes to planning the menu.

- If serving hot foods, prepare them so they can be heated in batches, with a constant rotation of warm foods at the ready.

- Mostly offer foods that do well at room temperature and require nothing more than a quick refresh and replenish.

- Avoid the need for utensils whenever possible. Fingers and cocktail napkins are all that should be required.

- Keep decorating to a minimum and focus on one key area, like the buffet table and bar.

- Embrace the use of disposable plates, cutlery and napkins.

- If you're hosting an evening event, don't forget to offer decaf coffee to your guests in addition to a regular variety.

- Empty your coat closet, leaving it free for your friends to hang their jackets themselves. If you don't have the space, store the jackets in another room and direct guests to where they can find their coats themselves.

- Make sure the second wave of visitors doesn't arrive to empty platters and warm punch; do a quick glance around the room every hour or so, bulking up the food, tidying the buffet, refilling the punch bowl and tossing crumbled cocktail napkins away.

NATURAL HOME FRESHENERS

When the temperature turns, and the days are cold, dark and grey, it's easy to add a cozy, welcoming scent to your home by creating natural air fresheners using common ingredients you likely tucked away in your kitchen. Combine favourite scented ingredients like vanilla and cinnamon, lemon and rosemary, or orange peel and clove in a pot, cover with water, bring to a boil and simmer on the stovetop until the water evaporates.

Other scents to try:

- vanilla and orange

- pink peppercorn and cinnamon

- pink grapefruit and thyme

- lemon and lavender

- juniper and peppercorn

- lime, mint and vanilla

MISTLETOE MOJITO PUNCH

Punch is fun, festive, inexpensive and always popular at a party. This version combines the minty and refreshing taste of a mojito, and pairs it with pomegranate and cranberries, decidedly two of the most popular flavours of the holiday season.

½ cup (125 mL) water

½ cup (125 mL) sugar

2 sprigs fresh mint leaves

½ cup (125 mL) lime juice

2½ cups (625 mL) cranberry juice

2½ cups (625 mL) pomegranate juice

1½ cups (375 mL) white rum

pomegranate seeds, mint leaves and lime slices, for garnish

ice

- Combine the water and sugar in a small saucepan and bring to a boil, whisking until the sugar is dissolved. Add the mint leaves and cook for 1 minute. Remove the pot from the heat and allow the mint to steep for 20 minutes. Discard the mint and, using a fine mesh sieve, strain syrup into a jar. Let cool completely.

- Fill a large glass pitcher or punch bowl with ice, and add the minted syrup, lime juice, cranberry juice, pomegranate juice and rum, stirring well. Just before serving, garnish with pomegranate seeds, mint leaves and lime slices.

PARTY POINTER To make this punch kid-friendly and non-alcoholic replace the rum with lemonade. If making both versions, include a "spiked" label on the punch with the rum. The minty simple syrup can be made up to a week ahead of time and stored in the fridge until needed.

Makes about 8 cups (2 L)

PUNCH BOWL POSSIBILITIES

If you don't have a punch bowl, or know of one that you can borrow, here are a few suggestions for other household items that can easily double as a basin for your beverage:

- trifle dish
- large stainless steel, glass, ceramic or enamelware serving bowl
- large glass canisters
- clean or new fish bowl
- soup pot
- Dutch oven
- slow cooker pot
- clean or new galvanized steel or plastic buckets
- glazed terra cotta plant pots (ensure drainage hole is plugged)
- soup tureen
- large fruit with thick shells, such as watermelons and pumpkins

CRANBERRY-ORANGE BOURBON COCKTAIL

If I'm asking you to purchase a bottle of bourbon for the apricot glaze in the ham recipe (Sticky Apricot Glazed Ham, page 163), I figure the least I can do is give you a way to use up the remainder in a seasonal cocktail. Make this fruit-infused drink up to two weeks or so before a party and consider offering it as a welcome drink to your friends when they arrive.

2 cups (500 mL) fresh or frozen cranberries

2 strips of 2-inch (5 cm) thick orange zest

2 cups (500 mL) bourbon

sparkling water, seltzer or ginger ale

- Combine the cranberries, orange zest and bourbon in a 1 qt (1 L) lidded jar. Store in the fridge for 3 days, shaking daily. Strain and discard fruit and keep chilled for up to 2 weeks. To serve, pour into a glass filled with ice and top with sparkling water, seltzer or ginger ale.

Makes 2 cups (500 mL)

STICKY APRICOT-GLAZED HAM

This is one dish that seems to go over well with everyone, and will leave you wondering why you don't make it more often. Relegated to special occasions and seasonal gatherings, ham works just as well for cocktail parties and Sunday suppers as it does for Easter dinner and holiday open houses. I like to place my ham on a wooden carving board with all of the accompaniments, letting my guests serve themselves when the time is right. Also, the meat tastes just as good regardless of whether you serve it hot or at room temperature.

one 6–7 lb (2.7–3.2 kg) bone-in, cured ham

1 cup (250 mL) apricot jam

½ cup (125 mL) bourbon or spiced rum

2 Tbsp (30 mL) grainy Dijon mustard

2 Tbsp (30 mL) brown sugar

- Preheat the oven to 350°F (175°C), with the rack placed at the lowest level possible.

- If the ham comes with a rind, remove it; using a sharp knife, trim the fat, leaving a ½-inch (1.5 cm) thick layer intact. Score the fat in a diamond pattern, taking care not to cut into the meat. Place the ham, fat side up, in a roasting pan lined with aluminum foil and bake for 1 hour.

- Meanwhile, combine the glaze ingredients in a medium saucepan set over medium heat, and cook, whisking until it starts to bubble. Reduce heat to a simmer and cook, stirring occasionally until syrupy, about 5 minutes.

- Remove ham from the oven and brush with the glaze. Return it to the oven and bake for another hour (or until a thermometer inserted into the thickest part of the meat registers 130°F [54°C]), basting with the glaze every 15 minutes. If the glaze starts to burn tent the ham with buttered foil.

- Remove ham from the oven and let rest for 20–30 minutes. Place on a platter or wooden carving board and serve with assorted mustard, cornichons and floury dinner rolls or biscuits (see Cheddar Biscuits, page 183, or Sweet Potato Biscuits, page 202).

Serves 8–12

TESS'S WARM AND SPICY SKILLET OLIVES

My good friend Tess is one of the best cooks I know, and she is constantly throwing new ideas my way. This is one of her back-pocket entertaining recipes, which just so happens to work equally as well in the summer as it does in the winter. Feel free to use lemon in place of the orange or clementines, and in the summer add a sprig or two of rosemary or thyme to the skillet for a pleasing herby addition to the dish.

3 cups (750 mL) mixed olives

⅔ cup (160 mL) olive oil

1 shallot, peeled, halved and thinly sliced

2 cloves garlic, minced

1 small red pepper, finely chopped

zest of 1 orange or 2 clementines

pinch red pepper flakes

1 baguette, cut into ½-inch (1 cm) thick slices

- Combine the olives, olive oil, shallot, garlic, red pepper and clementine pieces and zest in a medium mixing bowl and stir well to combine.

- Just before serving, warm a cast-iron skillet over medium heat. Dump the olive mixture into the pan and cook until the olives are warmed through and fragrant. Season with red pepper flakes and serve with slices of crusty baguette.

PARTY POINTER Make sure you provide a small bowl beside the skillet for olive pits.

Serves 6–8

CHEESY CHRISTMAS TREE

Pass on the customary cheese tray and build your own cheesy Christmas tree instead. The tree can be assembled at least one day in advance of serving. To store, cover loosely with a paper towel and wrap in plastic wrap. Feel free to use any variety of cheeses you like, alternating the flavours in each row.

3 or 4 different cheeses, cut into assorted 1-inch (2.5 cm) cubes

green grapes on vine

red grapes on vine

3 or 4 sprigs of rosemary

1 pretzel rod

1 slice cheddar cheese (for topper)

snowflake or star cookie cutter

- Arrange your cheese cubes into a triangular tree shape, breaking up the different varieties of cheese with a bunch of grapes and a sprig or 2 of rosemary.

- Snap the pretzel rod in half and make a tree trunk using the pieces. Using a star or snowflake-shaped cookie cutter, cut a cheese tree topper from the single piece of cheddar cheese and place at the top of the tree.

- Serve with assorted shaped and flavoured crackers.

PARTY POINTER Keep a container of extra cheese (pre-cubed) in the fridge and replenish the tree as needed.

Serves as many as needed

SWEET AND SPICY MIXED NUTS

This fail-safe finger food is one that everybody enjoys. Easily prepared, these nuts can be made far in advance of the holidays and stored in the freezer until needed.

1 egg white

2 cups (500 mL) mixed nuts (cashews, almonds, walnuts, pecans, peanuts)

¼ cup (60 mL) granulated sugar

¼ cup (60 mL) brown sugar

1 Tbsp (15 mL) cinnamon

½ tsp (2.5 mL) cumin

½ tsp (2.5 mL) coarse salt

pinch cayenne pepper

- Preheat the oven to 325°F (160°C) and line a baking sheet with parchment paper.
- Place egg white in a medium mixing bowl and beat until frothy; add nuts and toss to coat.
- Combine the sugar, cinnamon, cumin, salt and cayenne in a plastic zip-top bag and shake to mix. Add the nuts, seal the bag and shake vigorously, until the nuts are completely coated with the spice mixture.
- Spread the nuts in a single layer on the prepared baking sheet and bake for 20 minutes, stirring once halfway through the cooking time.
- Cool completely and break nuts apart if stuck together. Store in a tightly covered jar for up to 2 weeks, or in the freezer for 2 months.

Makes 2 cups (500 mL)

PRETZEL PARTY STICKS

Using only three ingredients, this party favourite goes quickly, so be sure to make plenty, especially if you have lots of little kids in attendance. Pretzel rods can usually be found in major supermarkets, cake decorating stores and in the baking section of major craft supply shops. Feel free to use any colour of chocolate you desire and get creative with your toppings by using a variety of sprinkles and small pieces of candy.

1 cup (250 mL) chocolate candy melts

One 10 oz (285 g) pkg pretzel rods

Assorted decorations like sprinkles and small or chopped candy

- Line a baking sheet with parchment paper and set aside.

- Melt the chocolate in the microwave, in 20-second intervals, or in a heatproof bowl set over simmering water, stirring occasionally, until smooth and glossy.

- Dip the ends of the pretzels into the pot, covering at least ⅓ of each stick with the melted chocolate. Decorate with sprinkles or candy pieces and lay the sticks on the parchment paper, allowing the chocolate to set at room temperature. Store in an airtight container for up to 1 week.

Makes 20 pieces

AUNT KATHY'S PEANUT BUTTER BALLS

Nothing has tastes like Christmas more than my Aunt Kathy's beloved peanut butter balls. These salty sweet treats were a staple around our holiday dinner table growing up, and our entire family would eagerly wait for her to pass out her tins of candy each December. Although I consumed more than my fair share over the years, I wasn't aware they contained bits of chopped dates and walnuts until she emailed me her secret recipe nearly a decade ago. Although she's no longer here to make them for us, I channel her to my kitchen every Christmas as I prepare a batch for my own friends and family. I really can't imagine a holiday party without them on the menu.

2 cups (500 mL) icing sugar

1 cup (250 mL) chopped pitted dates (preferably Medjool)

1 cup (250 mL) chopped walnuts

2 cups (500 mL) peanut butter

3 Tbsp (45 mL) butter, softened

16 oz (475 g) semi-sweet baking chocolate

1 tsp (5 mL) solid coconut oil or vegetable shortening

- In a large bowl combine the icing sugar, dates, walnuts, peanut butter and butter; mix well.

- Using your hands, roll the mixture into 1-inch (2.5 cm) balls. Place them on a parchment-lined baking sheet and chill for at least 1 hour.

- Fill a small saucepan with 2 inches (5 cm) of water. Place the chocolate and coconut oil in a heatproof bowl and set over the pot. Bring the water to a boil, reduce the heat to a simmer and warm the chocolate. When half of it has melted, remove the bowl from the heat, and stir until completely smooth.

- Using a fork, dip the peanut butter balls into the chocolate shaking the excess off onto the side of the bowl. Return the balls to the parchment lined baking sheet and place them in the freezer for 3–4 minutes, or long enough for the chocolate to firm up. Store in an airtight container in the fridge for up to 2 weeks. Alternatively, they can also be frozen. To serve, place the balls in mini cupcake liners, if desired.

PARTY POINTER Peanut butter balls can be made to look more festive by adding gold sanding sugar, chopped peanuts or silver dragées to the top of each piece of candy before the chocolate hardens.

Makes 40 peanut butter balls

HOW TO FEED A CROWD

One of the biggest obstacles any host can face is figuring out how much food to prepare for the number of people expected. There is no fool-proof formula, of course, and there are a series of things you need to consider before you begin planning an event, such as the type of food you'll be serving, the breakdown of guests (the ratio of men, women and children) and the start time of the party. A post-dinner cocktail requires less food then a gathering that begins at 4:00pm (your friends will likely be looking for dinner). It sounds complicated, but it isn't, and if you use the lists on page 175 you'll be able to figure out how much of each item you need in no time.

When deciding what type of food I want to serve I always keep my crowd in mind. I usually have a good grasp of my guests' palate preferences, making it easy to know which dishes will go over well, and which should be tucked away for another occasion. Once I've made a list of the foods I want to serve, I anticipate which dish will be the most popular, and make a large serving of that. For example, shrimp is almost always a crowd pleaser, so I serve as many pieces as my budget will allow.

When it comes to the guests, I like to keep in mind that if I've invited mostly men to my place I may need to increase the suggested quantities by half. If it's ladies I'm entertaining, I work with the amounts listed in the chart, but always expect to have a little leftover. If teenage boys are part of my crowd, I count each one as two eating adults, and anyone under the age of twelve usually consumes half of what a fully-grown person might eat.

Lastly, if you don't want to offer your friends a full meal, don't host them between 11:30am and 1:30pm, or between 4:00pm–7:00pm, otherwise you will be expected to serve a proper spread. Any other time of day requires nothing but munchies and snacks, unless of course, you want to put out more food, which is totally fine.—JS

FOOD QUANTITIES

The list below should serve as an approximate guideline for how much food you'll need at your cocktail and dinner parties.

SNACKS AND STARTERS

- 4–6 pieces/bites per person per hour (before a meal)

- 12–14 pieces/bites per person (as a meal)

- For hors d'oeuvres or appetizers not served in pieces (such as cheese), estimate 1 oz (30 g) per serving.

- Bulk items like chips and dips usually amount to 4–6 pieces/bites per person

SOUPS AND SALADS

- 8 oz (240 mL) soup per person (starter)

- 1½–2 cups (375–500 mL) soup per person (main meal)

- 1 cup (250 mL) salad per person (starter)

- 2–3 cups (500–750 mL) salad per person (main meal)

MAIN MEAL

- 6–8 oz (175–240 g) meat/protein per person

- 5–7 large shrimp per person

- 1 cup (250 mL) of each side/starch/grain per person

- 1½ dinner rolls per person

DESSERTS/SWEETS

- Assorted squares and cookies: 3 per person

- Cake/Pie: 1 piece per person

- Creamy desserts (pudding, mousse, etc.): ½–¾ cup (125–185 mL) per person

- Ice cream: ⅔ cup (160 mL) per person

BIG FAMILY *Gathering*

I LOVE BIG family gatherings—even when those around the table aren't related to me. Most families gather at least once a year, and while it's often Christmas that brings them all together, it could be a birthday or anniversary, a family reunion or just a case of everyone being in the same place at the same time.

Whatever the occasion, a large extended family—and perhaps a few extras—means varying ages and dietary needs, which can be a challenge to feed. Pork shoulder is a great cut for large groups; it's an inexpensive yet flavourful piece of meat, and requires little preparation or monitoring. A long, slow cooking time breaks down tough connective tissues, making it meltingly tender and easy to eat—no knife and fork required. Family and friends can serve themselves a lot or a little, and pulled pork will stay warm for hours without drying out. For really large crowds, it's the same amount of work to make a larger roast, or to cook two alongside each other, and if you go overboard (I always do) leftovers freeze beautifully. Serve pulled pork straight from the pot, or set your slow cooker right on the buffet table if it's a casual affair. Soft white buns are perfect for serving, but I love piling mine high on a cheddar biscuit; in fact, I've been known to make smaller versions for a cocktail party, cutting 1-inch (2.5 cm) rounds of biscuit dough, baking, splitting, then serving open-faced, with a small pile of pulled pork topped with a smaller one of creamy coleslaw.—JVR

THE LOGISTICS OF FEEDING A CROWD

One issue many of us have when faced with an overflowing house is where to sit everyone. We all know the card table scenario; if you don't have an extra folding table (or there are too many kids to seat at one), consider two sittings— feed the kids first, then shoo them off to play while the grown-ups eat. Or consider a buffet with food that requires no more than a fork to eat, making it easier to dine whilst sitting on the couch, standing in the hall or hanging out wherever your guests are most comfortable.

PULLED PORK

Pulled pork can be braised in the oven or done in a slow cooker. Whichever you choose, once pulled apart and moistened with barbecue sauce, it will stay warm for hours (whether in a cast iron pot in a low oven or in the slow cooker set on warm) without drying out.

one 3–5 lb (1.75–2.25 kg) pork shoulder

2 Tbsp (30 mL) chili powder

2 Tbsp (30 mL) brown sugar

½ tsp (2.5 mL) cumin

salt and pepper

canola oil, for cooking

2 onions, halved and thinly sliced

2 cups (500 mL) chicken stock, apple juice or beer

bottled barbecue sauce

soft white buns or cheddar biscuits

- Pat the pork shoulder dry with paper towels and rub it all over with the chili powder, brown sugar, cumin and plenty of salt and pepper. (If you like, do this up to a day in advance of cooking and keep it wrapped in the fridge.)

- In a large, heavy, ovenproof pot or if using slow cooker a large pan, heat a generous drizzle of oil over medium-high heat and brown the pork shoulder on all sides; set it aside on a plate or transfer to a slow cooker. Add the onions to the pot and cook, stirring to loosen the browned bits on the bottom of the pot, for 4–5 minutes, until golden.

- Return the pork to the pot if you're going to braise it. If you're using a slow cooker, put the onions in it and pour some of the stock into the pan to loosen any remaining browned bits; pour over the pork and onions in the slow cooker. Otherwise, add the stock to the pot, cover and roast at 300°F (150°C) for 3 hours, until the pork is very tender. Alternatively, cover the slow cooker and cook on low for 6–8 hours.

- Pull the meat apart with two forks and add enough barbecue sauce to moisten. Serve on cheddar biscuits, with creamy coleslaw if you like, and with extra barbecue sauce to pass at the table.

Serves 10–12

CHEDDAR BISCUITS

Everyone should know how to make a biscuit. With cheese baked inside, these are perfect for serving alongside soups and stews, or for splitting and stuffing with pulled pork. The recipe is easily doubled to serve an even larger crowd.

2 cups (500 mL) all-purpose flour

1 Tbsp (15 mL) baking powder

¼ tsp (1 mL) salt

½ cup (125 mL) butter, chilled and cut into pieces

½–1 cup (125–250 mL) grated old cheddar

¾ cup (185 mL) milk or buttermilk

- Preheat the oven to 425°F (220°C).

- In a large bowl (or in the bowl of a food processor) stir together the flour, baking powder and salt; add the butter and pulse or stir with a wire whisk or fork until well combined and crumbly. If you're using a food processor, transfer the mixture to a bowl. Add the cheese and toss to combine.

- Add the milk and stir until the dough comes together. For wedge-shaped biscuits, pat the dough into a circle that is about 1-inch (2.5 cm) thick on a parchment-lined baking sheet; cut the circle into 8 wedges and separate them so that they are at least an inch apart. For round biscuits, pat the dough about 1-inch (2.5 cm) thick and cut it into rounds with a biscuit cutter, glass rim or open end of a can, gently re-rolling the scraps.

- Bake for about 20 minutes, until golden.

Makes 8–12 biscuits

REAL BAKED BEANS

There's nothing like a pot of real baked beans to warm up the house, especially when served as a side dish to pulled pork. Best of all, both dishes can be baked alongside one another, so both will be ready to eat at the same time. Alternatively, you can prepare these beans in a slow cooker on low for six to eight hours.

1½ cups (375 mL) dry white beans

1 onion, finely chopped

¾ cup (185 mL) ketchup

¾ cup (185 mL) barbecue sauce

1 cup (250 mL) beer, apple juice or chicken stock

¼ cup (60 mL) packed dark brown sugar

¼ cup (60 mL) apple cider vinegar

2 Tbsp (30 mL) yellow or grainy mustard

- Put the dry beans in a large saucepan and add enough water to cover by a couple inches. Set aside to soak for 8 hours, or overnight.

- Add the onion to the pot and bring to a simmer over medium-high heat; cook for 45 minutes, or until the beans are just tender.

- Drain off the water and put the beans and onion in a baking dish. Preheat the oven to 325°F (160°C). Add the remaining ingredients to the pot, stir well to combine, cover and bake for 2–3 hours, stirring once or twice, until the mixture is thick and sticky and the beans are very tender.

Serves 8

BOURBON ROASTED PEACHES WITH VANILLA ICE CREAM

Warm bourbon roasted peaches require minimal prep and taste divine served warm over vanilla ice cream. Leave the bourbon out of the recipe if there are kids at the table; leftover roast peaches can, on the other hand, be packed into a jar and covered with more bourbon if you like, to store in the fridge. To dress up dessert a little further, crumble store-bought shortbread cookies over your sundaes as well, or pile everything onto a slab of cake. This recipe can easily be multiplied to feed a larger crowd or to produce leftovers.

6 peaches, pitted and halved

½ cup (125 mL) brown sugar

¼ cup (60 mL) butter, melted

2-4 Tbsp (30-60 mL) bourbon (optional)

vanilla ice cream, for serving

shortbread cookies, crumbled (optional)

- Preheat the oven to 425°F (220°C).

- Place the peaches cut side up on a parchment-lined rimmed baking sheet. Sprinkle with brown sugar and drizzle with butter and bourbon, if you're using it.

- Roast for 20–30 minutes, until the peaches are soft and starting to turn golden on the edges. Remove from the oven and serve over (or under) a scoop of vanilla ice cream, with the extra juices from the bottom of the pan drizzled over top. If you like, crumble some shortbread cookies over top, too.

Serves 6–12

HOW TO ENTERTAIN IN A SMALL SPACE

There are many reasons why people refrain from casual entertaining at home, but one of the most unnecessary is a perceived lack of available space, which hosts and hostesses fear is preventing them from comfortably accommodating their friends. It's disheartening to think that there are folks out there holding back from gathering with dear ones simply because they feel there isn't enough room to have friends and family over to share a meal.

I've never lived in a home blessed with ample space, and to be completely honest, it has never bothered me. From a 400 sq. foot bachelor apartment to a small two-bedroom urban house, all of our homes have been small in size, and I really kind of prefer it that way, despite the challenges that come with packing a family and a few pets into cramped quarters. Thankfully, our lack of space has never placed limits on our ability to entertain, even in that too-tiny apartment back when we were childless adults learning our way around a kitchen, and we've been fairly creative when it comes to feeding a crowd in our space ever since.

- If you're feeling short on space consider maximizing serving surfaces by going vertical—use cake stands and tiered platters to elevate food, which will allow you to squeeze more into a small area. If you don't have cake stands, set a pretty plate on top of an inverted wine or water glass and voila—an instant serving stand.

- If you have decorations at your party, hang them from the walls and ceilings in order to keep tabletops and counters free—you'll need those for drinks and food, not to mention as somewhere for people to put their feet up in relaxation.

CONTINUED . . .

- Why not take the party outside whenever possible? There's almost always more space outdoors, allowing people to move about and mingle. From early spring to late fall it's entirely possible to gather your guests in your backyard or on your balcony, where you can serve them something to eat outdoors. In cooler temperatures you can offer cozy blankets, make a fire if you have a portable fire pit, or eat earlier during the day when the sun is at it's warmest.

- Be open to rearranging the furniture if it's necessary. Move an end table to another room, or place a large floor plant in your bedroom; push sofas and chairs against walls around the perimeter of the room, opening up the floor space for easy movement and additional seating.

- It's worth keeping in mind that folding tables and chairs create non-permanent seating and dining options that can easily be tucked away under beds or sofas, stored in a basement or garage or hidden in the back of a closet up against a wall. A coffee table and throw cushions can easily double for a dining space when you have a small group over.

- If you don't have enough seating for all of your guests serve the food buffet-style, which automatically signals that the meal is a more casual affair. Guests can help themselves to a plate of food and find a spot to sit or stand wherever there is space. No need to fuss with place settings, just make sure everyone has a decent napkin and the utensils required for the meal they're eating.

- Tidy small spaces like tables, mantles and bookcases, clearing away everyday items like books, magazines, remote controls, etc. in order to create small spots for people to put down glasses and plates.

- While it's fine to set out a central buffet of foods for people to choose from, make sure that each conversation hub has something to pick from as well. I like the idea of adding small bowls of nuts, olives, chips and popcorn to the corners of a room for my friends to nibble on while chatting with other guests. This will keep guests from having to continuously walk around the area, cluttering up the corners and hallways.

- I don't believe in buying furniture just for the purposes of entertaining—if you don't have a sideboard, clear a shelf on your bookcase for the champagne bucket and nibbles, making an ad hoc self-serve bar area.

- Store small appliances in a cupboard, closet or another room leaving lots of counter space for meal prep and/or a buffet.

- If you have kids coming to your place and there isn't enough space to seat them with the adults, set up a kid's table in another room, like a basement playroom, kitchen or, if the weather is nice, on the patio. Kids don't notice the cold quite like the adults, and even in the winter they would be delighted to bundle up and eat at a picnic table in the snow.

- Clear space in your coat closet to hang you guest's jackets. Move your items to a bedroom closet for the night so your friends' coats can be hung. If you don't have a coat closet, revert to the old-fashioned method of storing jackets on a bed. No one will mind and you can even have older kids create a ticket system and be in charge of collecting the coats at the end of the evening.—JS

FALL HARVEST *Dinner*

THE FIRST TIME I told my extended family that our annual Thanksgiving dinner was to be held outdoors, there was no mistaking the "you've lost your mind, lady" look that crossed almost every face in the room. I had wanted to celebrate the day of Thanks outside for a few years at that point, but every October had arrived with uncertain weather forecasts, forcing me to hold the event indoors. Happily, nearly five years later our annual outdoor Thanksgiving has become a ritual success, thanks in no small part to the glorious October weather that's graced us each year. I dare say it's now a holiday feast the entire family looks forward to, especially so given the size of our smallish dining room and the issue of our family tripling in size over the past decade. As each Thanksgiving Sunday arrives with bright blue skies and a warm welcoming temperature, I revel in the decision to start dining al fresco.

Of course, serving poultry outdoors isn't always a possibility given the conditions and preparations a Thanksgiving feast requires, and in recent years I've been drawn to the idea of hosting an outdoor harvest dinner as an alternative. Unlike our traditional open-air holiday gathering, a harvest celebration is easier to execute simply because it's not tied to a specific date on the calendar or those time-honoured dishes that require copious co-operation and an abundance of planning. This type of meal works well for everything from milestone birthdays to post-apple picking outings, and should be straightforward, seasonal and prepared without too much fuss, letting the ingredients speak for themselves. It's a chance to connect with friends and family in a casual setting, bridging the gap between summer salads and barbecues and classic comfort foods served indoors by the fire.—JS

PULLING OFF THE PERFECT OUTDOOR HARVEST DINNER

Anyone who's hosted an outdoor wedding knows that the most essential ingredient to a successful day is to come equipped with a solid back-up plan. The same can be said for a simple outdoor harvest dinner; if you have to bring your guests indoors, know exactly where they're going to sit and how the food will be served.

Elements of surprise in a menu are nice, but the meal at an outdoor dinner should be straightforward and seasonal, prepared without too much fuss. Take advantage of the bounty that's available in your area in the fall, and prepare simple food that will allow you to spend more time with your guests.

If you prefer to enjoy the warm afternoon sunshine, consider an early dinner hour by suggesting guests arrive at 3:00pm, with dinner scheduled for 4:00pm. Tables should be placed where the sun will be brightest, in order to ward off a late afternoon or early evening chill.

Outdoor dinners lend themselves well to creative table settings because the main décor is the scenery surrounding the celebration. Mix and match rustic tables and comfortable chairs, use hay bales for additional seating, dress tables with squashes in assorted colours, sizes and shapes, and coax guests into lingering for a little longer by hanging twinkling lights over and around the table.

Plan lots of fun for the kids in attendance. Seek inspiration from your favourite fall fairs and farms and organize a little kid-friendly, outdoor excitement (see Games and Activities for an Outdoor Harvest Dinner, page 206).

PORK TENDERLOIN WITH MAPLE BALSAMIC AND CRANBERRY SAUCE

Pork tenderloin is one of the easiest proteins to cook and can work as well for a quick week-night dinner as it can for feeding a large group of friends. It pairs perfectly with most fruits and a variety of spices, and the only thing you ever need to worry about is overcooking the meat, which can transform this dish from tender to tough in just a few minutes.

FOR THE MARINADE

1 cup (250 mL) maple syrup

1 cup (250 mL) balsamic vinegar

2 Tbsp (30 mL) Dijon mustard

juice and zest of 1 orange

1 Tbsp (15 mL) fresh rosemary, finely chopped

FOR THE PORK TENDERLOIN

2 pork tenderloins
(3–4 lb [1.4–1.8 kg] total)

salt and pepper

½ cup (125 mL) red wine

1 Tbsp (15 mL) butter

1 Tbsp (15 mL) olive oil

1 cup (250 mL) fresh or frozen cranberries

- To make the marinade, whisk together the maple syrup, balsamic vinegar, Dijon mustard, orange juice and zest, and the rosemary.

- Place the tenderloins in a shallow baking dish and season all sides well with salt and pepper. Combine ½ cup (125 mL) marinade with the red wine and pour over the meat. Cover tightly with plastic wrap and refrigerate for 2–4 hours, turning occasionally.

- Preheat the oven to 400°F (200°C). Place a large ovenproof skillet over medium-high heat and add the butter and olive oil. When the butter has melted, sear the tenderloins on all sides until well browned. Transfer the skillet to the oven and cook for 15 minutes or until the meat reaches an internal temperature of 155–160°F (68–71°C).

- Remove the pork from the skillet and transfer to a cutting board. Cover with foil and let rest for 10 minutes.

- Meanwhile, place the skillet on the stove over medium heat and whisk in the remaining maple balsamic marinade, scraping up the browned bits from the bottom of the pan as you stir; they provide plenty of flavour for the sauce. Add the cranberries and bring the sauce to a boil. Reduce the heat to medium low and cook, stirring occasionally until thick and syrupy, about 10 minutes.

- Slice the pork into 1-inch (2.5 cm) thick slices and spoon the glaze over the meat, or serve it on the side in a small pitcher.

Serves 4–6

POTATOES DAUPHINOISE

This classic dish with tender potatoes and a caramelized crust is a crowd-pleasing comfort food that pairs well with most meats. You can also serve it as a vegetarian main course alongside a simple green salad and French lentils, or even with a colourful ratatouille.

1 Tbsp (15 mL) butter

3 cups (750 mL) heavy (whipping) cream

2 garlic cloves, smashed with the side of a knife blade but not chopped

2–3 sprigs fresh thyme

salt and pepper

fresh ground nutmeg

3 lb (1.4 kg) Yukon gold or russet potatoes

1 cup (250 mL) grated Parmesan cheese

- Preheat the oven to 350°F (175°C) and grease a 9 × 9-inch (23 × 23 cm) or similar-sized casserole dish with the butter.

- Place the cream in a large pot with the garlic cloves, thyme sprigs and 1 tsp (5 mL) salt, warming over medium-high just until bubbles begin to form around the edge of the pot. Reduce heat to low and simmer for 10 minutes. Remove from the heat and set aside, discarding the garlic and thyme.

- Ladle a small amount of the seasoned cream in the bottom of the baking dish. Add a layer of potatoes, overlapping slightly and spread evenly over the pan; season with a pinch of nutmeg and sprinkling of salt and fresh ground pepper. Spoon a layer of cream over top, and repeat with the remaining ingredients, alternating layers of potatoes, nutmeg, salt and pepper and seasoned cream. When finished, pour any excess cream over the top, shaking the casserole dish around to distribute the cream evenly. Cover with aluminum foil and bake for 1½ hours.

- Remove the foil, top the potatoes with the Parmesan cheese and bake for an additional 25–35 minutes, or until the top is golden and bubbly, and a small knife slides easily into the centre of the potatoes. Let stand for at least 10 minutes before serving.

1. Substitute 1 medium sweet potato and 1 small butternut squash for half the potatoes.

2. Top each layer of potatoes with ¼ cup (60 mL) caramelized onions and ¼ cup (60 mL) shredded cheddar cheese before covering with the cream.

Serves 6

ROASTED BRUSSELS SPROUTS WITH WALNUTS AND GRAINY MUSTARD SAUCE

This recipe is indebted to a memorable plate of Brussels sprouts my husband and I once salivated over whilst out on an exceptionally appetizing date night. Even though they preceded a truly decadent dinner of grilled pizza and local beer, Brussels sprouts were all we could talk about on the walk home, and I concocted this recipe in tribute to that mouthwatering menu item. Completely different from the mushy morsels we remember from our youth, these caramelized and slightly crunchy cruciferous veggies appear frequently on our dinner table, and we've converted quite a few people to this version of a restaurant favourite.

8 cups (2 L) Brussels sprouts

olive oil

salt and pepper

2 Tbsp (30 mL) honey

2 Tbsp (30 mL) grainy Dijon mustard

½ cup (125 mL) walnuts, roughly chopped

- Preheat oven to 425°F (220°C).

- Slice ends off of the bottoms of the sprouts and cut each sprout in half. Remove the outer leaves and the toss the rest onto a large, rimmed baking sheet, separating some of the leaves from the core.

- Add a few large glugs of olive oil, and season well with sea salt and lots of fresh ground pepper, massaging the oil and spices into the sprouts. Place the cut sides down on the pan and bake for 12–15 minutes, or until the leaves are a dark amber colour and the cores are nicely caramelized.

- Combine the honey and grainy Dijon mustard in a small bowl. Transfer the cooked veggies to a serving bowl, add the walnuts, drizzle the mustard sauce over and gently toss to combine.

PARTY POINTER This dish is amazing as is, but for fun I like to replace the walnuts with chopped up bits of leftover ham (not the deli kind) and serve as a side for pizza night (see Pizza Party, page 121). The sprouts can be roasted up to 6 hours in advance and gently warmed before serving.

Serves 6–8

MIXED GREENS SALAD WITH PUMPKIN SEEDS AND PARMESAN

This salad is loosely based on one that I occasionally order at a local coffee shop. Whenever I come home I can't stop talking about how tasty it is, so I decided to make my own version and include apples, which are always abundant in the fall. Whisk up the vinaigrette before doing anything else; it will keep in the fridge for up to one week, so feel free to make it ahead of time. It also happens to taste great when tossed with roasted root vegetables and crumbled goat cheese, so I encourage you to give that a try sometime.

MAPLE DIJON VINAIGRETTE

1 tsp (5 mL) Dijon mustard

2 Tbsp (30 mL) balsamic vinegar

1 Tbsp (15 mL) + 1 tsp (5 mL) pure maple syrup

6 Tbsp (90 mL) canola or safflower oil

¼ tsp (1 mL) salt

¼ tsp (1 mL) pepper

SALAD

two 5 oz (150 g) containers mixed greens

⅔ cup (160 mL) dried cranberries

½ cup (125 mL) pumpkin seeds

⅓ cup (80 mL) finely diced red onion

2 tart apples, cored and diced

½ cup (125 mL) freshly shaved Parmesan cheese

- In a small bowl whisk together the Dijon mustard, balsamic vinegar and maple syrup. Slowly add the oil to the bowl, whisking as you go. Season with the salt and pepper; store in a jar and keep in the fridge for up to a week.

- Place the greens in a large salad bowl. Add the remaining ingredients and gently toss with the dressing just before serving.

Serves 8

SWEET POTATO BISCUITS

Sweet potatoes give these biscuits a fluffy texture and charming golden hue, and they look lovely on the plate when served with any fall-inspired meal. Leftovers can be sliced and stuffed with assorted meats like turkey or ham or even a fried egg for a fabulous homemade breakfast sandwich, which tastes especially great when slathered with sweet homemade Honey Cardamom Butter (see page 76).

1 large sweet potato, peeled and cubed

1 cup (250 mL) all-purpose flour, plus extra for dusting and cutting

¾ cup (185 mL) whole wheat flour

2 Tbsp (30 mL) dark brown sugar

1 Tbsp (15 mL) baking powder

½ tsp (2.5 mL) baking soda

½ tsp (2.5 mL) salt

½ tsp (2.5 mL) ground cumin or smoked paprika

½ cup (125 mL) unsalted butter, chilled and cut into ½-inch (1 cm) cubes

½ cup (125 mL) + 1 Tbsp (15 mL) cold buttermilk

- Place sweet potato pieces in a saucepan and cover with water. Season with salt and bring to a boil. Cook for 6–8 minutes or until tender. Drain, cool and mash into a puree.

- Preheat the oven to 425°F (220°C), and line a rimmed baking sheet with parchment paper.

- Whisk the flour, sugar, baking soda, baking powder, salt and cumin together in a medium mixing bowl. Add the butter to the flour mixture and work it in with your hands until the texture is coarse and sandy.

- Whisk ¾ cup (185 mL) of the mashed sweet potatoes with the buttermilk until smooth. Add to the flour mixture and stir together with a fork. Knead the dough until it comes together.

- Spread a small amount of flour onto the counter, place the dough ball on top of the flour and pat it out into a 1-inch (2.5 cm) thick circle. Using a floured cookie cutter or water glass, cut out biscuits and place them on the prepared baking sheet. Bake for 8 minutes or until tops are golden brown.

PARTY POINTER Keep packets of sweet potato puree (made following the instructions in the first step above) in the freezer, measured into ¾ cup (185 mL) portions and stored in a flattened freezer bag so you can make these easily whenever the mood strikes.

Makes 12 biscuits

PEAR AND CARDAMOM CREAM CHEESE TART

While traditionally used in savoury dishes, cardamom offers a fragrant dose of spice that pairs (pun intended!) perfectly with sweet pears and crunchy almonds, and which adds a definitive fall flavour to this rustic dessert. You can incorporate your favourite varieties of pear into this recipe, but I like to mix colours—red, green and brown—adding a little extra colour to the plate.

CRUST

1 cup (250 mL) all-purpose flour

½ tsp (2.5 mL) salt

⅓ cup (80 mL) icing sugar

½ cup (125 mL) cold unsalted butter, cut into small pieces

FILLING

one 8 oz (240 g) pkg cream cheese, at room temperature

¼ cup (60 mL) sugar

1 large egg

1 tsp (5 mL) vanilla

PEARS

¼ cup (60 mL) sugar

1 Tbsp (15 mL) lemon juice

5 pears, cored, peeled and sliced ¼-inch (0.6 cm) thick

½ tsp (2.5 mL) ground cardamom

½ cup (125 mL) sliced almonds

icing sugar

- Preheat the oven to 350°F (175°C) and place rack in the centre; grease a 9-inch (23 cm) spring form or tart pan. Set aside.

- To make the crust, place the flour, salt and sugar in the bowl of a food processor fitted with a steel blade, pulsing the ingredients until well combined. Add the butter and pulse just until the dough begins to come together. Spoon the dough onto the bottom of the spring form or tart pan and press evenly across the bottom and up the sides. Cover with plastic wrap and place in the refrigerator while you make the filling.

- To make the filling, place the cream cheese and sugar in the bowl of the washed food processor fitted with a steel blade and blend until smooth. Add the egg and vanilla and process until silky.

- Remove the crust from the fridge and pour the filling into the pan. Cover and return to the fridge while you prepare the topping.

- To make the topping, stir together the sugar and lemon juice in a medium mixing bowl. Add the pears and cardamom and toss to combine. Remove the base from the fridge and arrange the pear slices evenly over the cream cheese layer. Sprinkle with the almond slices.

- Bake for 25–30 minutes, or until the tart crust is golden brown and the filling is almost set. Place on a wire rack to cool.

- Lightly dust the tart with icing sugar and serve at room temperature.

Serves 6–8

SPICED MULLED WINE OR CIDER

This is my friend Shannon's famous mulled wine. She recommends using a dry red wine over a fruity variety, and feels the flavours really pop when some of the wine is reduced to a syrupy consistency, a tip she learned from Jamie Oliver. Feel free to replace the wine with apple cider for a non-alcoholic version of the same drink.

1 navel orange

one 1-inch (2.5 cm) piece lemon peel (for mulled wine only)

one 1-inch (2.5 cm) piece lime peel (2.5 cm) (for mulled wine only)

6–8 whole cloves

3–4 small (or 2 large broken) cinnamon sticks

3 fresh bay leaves

⅛ tsp (0.5 mL) freshly grated nutmeg

1 vanilla bean, split

2–3 whole star anise

2 cardamom pods

1 cup (250 mL) sugar (1½ cups [375 mL] if using 3 bottles of wine)

two or three 25 oz (750 mL) bottles red wine

OPTIONAL

¼ cup (60 mL) orange-flavoured liqueur or even brandy (for mulled wine only)

cinnamon sticks and orange slices, for garnish

- Peel and juice the orange. In a large pot, combine the citrus peels, the juice of the orange, all of the spices and the sugar. Set the mixture over medium heat and give it a few stirs, lightly toasting the ingredients to release some of the flavours.

- Add 1 cup (250 mL) of wine and stir continuously until the sugar is dissolved; add a little more wine, if needed. Turn the heat to high and bring the mixture to a boil, letting it bubble for 5 minutes, or until it becomes thick and syrupy.

- Reduce the heat to a simmer and add the rest of the wine. Stir and heat until warmed through. Add the liqueur, if using, and mix well. Turn off the heat and strain into glass tumblers. Serve with a cinnamon stick and orange slice.

PARTY POINTER Both variations of this recipe can be made ahead of time and stored in the fridge. Gently rewarm just before serving.

Serves a medium-sized crowd

GAMES AND ACTIVITIES FOR AN OUTDOOR HARVEST DINNER

Food is always the focus of our annual outdoor Thanksgiving dinner, but planning games for the kids to participate in is usually a close second. From butternut squash bowling to donut on a string, we take our inspiration from fall fairs and carnivals and set up at least three activities to keep the young ones excited and entertained.

BUTTERNUT SQUASH BOWLING

WHAT YOU NEED 5–10 butternut squash that stand upright and a round pumpkin with the stem removed.

HOW TO SET UP Stagger the squash in a 5 or 10 pin bowling formation so the gourds fall like dominos when hit.

WHAT TO DO Have kids take turns "bowling". They each get three attempts to knock down as many "pins" as they can. Keep score of how many squash get knocked over during the course of 5–10 (depending on the age of the kids) rounds. For an extra challenge, have kids take one step backwards during each turn, placing them farther away from the pins each time.

DONUTS ON A STRING

WHAT YOU NEED One donut per child (plain or powdered sugar work best) and string.

HOW TO SET UP Tie a length of string around the middle of each donut and hang them from the branches of a tree or a secure line of rope. Space the donuts at least 12 inches (30 cm) apart and hang them at various lengths to accommodate a variety of heights.

WHAT TO DO Players stand with their mouths close to the hanging donuts and their hands clasped behind their backs. The "judge" shouts, "Go!" and kids eat their donuts as quickly as possible without using their fingers. The first player to finish eating and chewing their donut wins. Play continues until all donuts have been consumed.

PRETZEL TOSS

WHAT YOU NEED Large floury pretzels and wooden dowels or sticks (one per child).

HOW TO SET UP Pair the kids up, partnering children who are of similar height together. Give each group one pretzel and each child one wooden dowel or stick.

WHAT TO DO Have one player place a pretzel on their stick and toss it into the air; their opponent needs to catch the pretzel on their stick, which will require some running around to do successfully. Note that this game can be a challenge for children under the age of 8.

PILLOW SACK RACES

WHAT YOU NEED One pillowcase or flour sack per every two kids, and rope or ribbon to create start and finish lines.

HOW TO SET UP Make a start line and finish line using the rope or ribbon. Divide the children into pairs or let them choose their own partner; provide each group with a pillowcase. Position all of the kids on the start line, explaining that each person must have at least one foot in their sack.

WHAT TO DO When everyone is ready blow a whistle or yell, "Go!" Pairs must hop, run, walk or jump down to the finish line keeping at least one leg each in the sack. The first pair to make it to the finish line is declared the winner and they can demonstrate their "technique" to the rest of the group, showing how they were able to move across the field so quickly.

APPLE BOBBING

WHAT YOU NEED Large buckets, tubs or bowls (one for each player) and a few apples per person. Also, it's handy to have chairs or low tables for the buckets, as the top of the basin should be at about waist-height for most players. Also required: towels for drying faces.

HOW TO SET UP Fill buckets three-quarters full of cool water. Float a few apples in the containers, but not too many, as you want to create a challenge for the players; place basins on chairs or tables.

WHAT TO DO Ask players to stand in front of a bucket with hands behind their backs. On "Go!" they place their face in the water and try to grab an apple with their teeth. The person who catches the first apple is declared the winner. Dry faces and play again.

SUNDAY *Supper*

BIG SUNDAY DINNERS are not as commonplace as they once were; our parents and grandparents most likely have memories of big family gatherings every Sunday afternoon or evening featuring a hefty chunk of roasted meat and a pitcher of gravy. I'm always trying to reignite that tradition and create those sorts of comforting memories since, as Mr. Carson once said in the PBS series *Downton Abbey,* "The business of life is the acquisition of memories; in the end that's all there is."

Even with busy schedules, Sundays still offer a weekly excuse to gather some of your favourite people around the table. If the thought of cooking for a large group is daunting, make it a potluck or assign dishes, taking charge of the main course yourself. If you want to go old-school, roast beef has been a Sunday dinner staple for generations, or if you want something more contemporary (but equally beefy) I recommend braised beef or bison short ribs. These are great for serving to large groups, and can spend the afternoon simmering to the point of almost falling off the bone while you toss a salad and set the table. (Meanwhile, if they need to vacate the oven to make way for Yorkshire puddings or a tartiflette, they're easy to keep warm without overcooking or drying out—just set over low heat on the stovetop.)

If you're not one for table setting or don't have any good china, try a simple table runner (even a strip of burlap running down the middle of the table adds a rustic look, as Jan taught me); with more mouths to feed, mismatched plates and cutlery add a certain charm if that's all you've got. To add a little inexpensive bling, snip a few big flowers—like hydrangeas, peonies or Gerbera daisies—and set out a single bloom of each in a few jars or glasses of water. (Not only are these easy to arrange, they won't get in the way of the food or obstruct vision of your dinner companions.) Add a few tea lights and Sunday's all set.—JVR

BRAISED BEEF OR BISON SHORT RIBS

Short, stocky beef or bison short ribs are often overlooked at the butcher shop, and yet they're among the most flavourful cuts available. Braising is a simple cooking method; the meat only needs to be browned and then cooked at a low temperature in the liquid of your choice—red wine, beer, tomato juice or stock. A splash of balsamic is delicious, and try adding a few springs of fresh rosemary or thyme. Dinner all but makes itself.

canola oil, for cooking

2 lb (1 kg) bison or beef short ribs (about 8)

salt and pepper

1 small onion, chopped (optional)

1 carrot, chopped (optional)

1 celery stalk, chopped (optional)

2 garlic cloves, crushed

¼ cup (60 mL) balsamic vinegar

1 cup (250 mL) red wine

beef or chicken stock (or more wine)

a few sprigs of fresh rosemary and/or thyme

- Heat a drizzle of oil in a heavy skillet or ovenproof pot set over medium-high heat. In the pot, season the ribs with salt and pepper and brown on all sides; set aside. Add the onion, carrot and celery to the pot, if you are using them, and cook for a few minutes until they start to soften; add the garlic and cook for another minute. Pour in the balsamic vinegar and cook for 1 minute, scraping up the browned bits from the bottom of the pan.

- Return the ribs to the pot. Pour the wine over top and add enough stock to come about halfway up the sides of the ribs. Toss in a few sprigs of rosemary and/or thyme.

- Cover and cook at 300°F (150°C) for 3 hours, until the meat is very tender. Pull out any sprigs of rosemary or the twigs leftover from the thyme. If you like, uncover and remove the ribs and simmer the sauce on the stovetop to reduce it slightly. Return the ribs to the pot and serve.

PARTY POINTER Braised short ribs require only potatoes (in any form) to catch flavourful drips, and they take care of their own gravy, so you can still justify pairing them with crunchy Yorkshire puddings. Add buttered carrots or green beans and a big salad. Leftover meat can be pulled off the bone and added to grilled cheese sandwiches, tacos or pasta sauce.

Serves 8

OTHER THINGS TO CONSIDER WHEN PLANNING YOUR MENU

- Don't repeat main ingredient items. For example, if you're serving beef as a part of your main meal, don't include it in your appetizers.

- When preparing a buffet, be sure to include both hot and cold items.

- Always consider colour when planning your menu, and make sure there is an ample amount in your dishes. Also, don't forget about the crunch factor—there should be a good variety of textures on your plate.

- Always have a handful of items on hand that don't require any cooking, like assorted breads and flatbreads, olive and nuts, pretzels and chips, etc. They add bulk to the menu and don't require a lot of effort to prepare.

WHAT ABOUT THE PARTY PICTURES?

In a perfect world, I'd be the type of host who could simultaneously make drinks, take coats, greet people at the door, serve food, engage in compelling conversations and take pictures at my party. Sadly, that's not the case, and at the end of a gathering I'm often wishing I had made more of an effort to pick-up the camera and capture at least one good decent keepsake photo.

It's always easy to ask other people to grab a few shots with their camera phones, but tracking down the pictures afterwards isn't always ideal or easy. As a result I've come up with another solution instead, which is to leave my camera within easy reach of almost everyone, and I ask my friends to take photos for me.

In an effort to make the task fun, and to ensure quality pictures worth keeping, I find it helpful to leave a list of prompts to encourage specific photos that I'll be glad to have after the party. They include, but aren't limited to:

- guests arriving
- drinks
- favourite food
- shoes
- the time
- the date
- something held
- someone you love
- something beginning with "S"
- a group of people
- guest of honour

- a pet
- hands/feet
- people laughing
- a smiling kid
- a self-portrait
- a candid shot of the host
- decorations
- dessert
- the mess
- the last person leaving

YORKSHIRE PUDDING

Classic Yorkshire pudding is made with a simple batter of eggs, milk and flour whisked together and baked in a hot pan until dramatically puffed, golden and crunchy. The trick is to heat the pan first, then pour in the batter before it cools down.

canola oil or lard, for cooking

3 large eggs

1 cup (250 mL) milk

1 cup (250 mL) all-purpose flour

pinch salt

- Preheat the oven to 450°F (230°C). Drizzle a little canola oil or lard into each cup of a metal muffin tin and put it in the oven as it heats.

- In a medium bowl, whisk together the eggs, milk, flour and salt until smooth. Remove the pan from the oven and pour about ¼ cup (60 mL) of the batter into each metal cup; return to the oven and bake for 20 minutes, until puffed and golden.

Makes about 1 dozen Yorkshire puddings

WHITE & SWEET POTATO TARTIFLETTE

A *tartiflette* is a Quebecois dish of roasted potatoes topped with a wheel of cheese; Aimee Nimbus-Bourque of *Simple Bites* taught me to make it with Oka, and I recently tried it with a combination of white and sweet potatoes. It's infinitely easier to make than scalloped potatoes, and the crispy, cheesy bits are irresistible. We set the whole cast iron pan on the table—and have been known to simply gather around the skillet with forks.

1 lb (500 g) russet or yellow-skinned potatoes, scrubbed and cut into 1-inch (2.5 cm) pieces

1 lb (500 g) dark-fleshed sweet potatoes, scrubbed and cut into 1-inch (2.5 cm) pieces

6 slices bacon, chopped

¾ cup (185 mL) heavy (whipping) cream or 18% coffee cream

1 small wheel Oka cheese

- Preheat oven to 350°F (175°C). In a medium pot, cover the potatoes with water and bring to a simmer; cook for 10–15 minutes, until just tender when poked with a fork, but still firm in the middle.

- In a large, heavy, ovenproof skillet, cook the bacon over medium-high heat until crisp; drain the potatoes well and add them to the skillet, stirring to combine everything well. Spread them out into a single layer and pour the cream evenly over top.

- Cut a thin slice off one flat side of the Oka and scratch the other side with a fork or tip of a knife. Place open side down on the potatoes and bake for 40–45 minutes, until the cheese is melted and the potatoes are golden, with lots of crispy bits. Serve immediately.

Serves 4–6

CHEESECAKE WITH HOT FUDGE SAUCE

This ultra-simple cheesecake can be made in advance; it lies in wait in the fridge until you're ready for it. You could top it with anything—like fresh fruit in season—or douse it in warm chocolate sauce spiked with coffee or chocolate liqueur, like Kahlua or Bailey's. If there are kids at the table, skip the espresso and booze and call it an Oreo cookie cheesecake (since it too has chocolate on both sides and a creamy middle).

CRUST

1½ cups (375 mL) chocolate cookie crumbs

1 Tbsp (15 mL) sugar

¼ cup (60 mL) butter, melted

FILLING

two 8 oz (240 g) pkg cream cheese, at room temperature

½ cup (125 mL) golden syrup or pure maple syrup

1 cup (250 mL) heavy (whipping) cream

2 Tbsp (30 mL) icing sugar

½ tsp (2.5 mL) vanilla

HOT FUDGE SAUCE

½ cup (125 mL) heavy (whipping) cream

2 Tbsp (30 mL) golden syrup or pure maple syrup

6 oz (175 mL) chopped dark or semi-sweet chocolate, or 1 cup (250 mL) chocolate chips

- To make the crust, preheat the oven to 350°F (175°C). Mix the cookie crumbs, sugar and butter in a small bowl until well blended; press into the bottom of an 8- or 9-inch (20 or 23 cm) springform pan. Bake for 10 minutes, until set; cool completely.

- To make the filling, beat the cream cheese in a large bowl for 2–3 minutes, until creamy and light; add the syrup and beat until well blended and smooth. In a medium bowl, beat the cream, icing sugar and vanilla until stiff peaks form. Add about a third of this to the cream cheese mixture and gently fold in with a spatula just until combined—streaks are OK. Add the remaining whipped cream and fold in just until combined. Spread onto the cooled crust, cover and refrigerate for several hours, or overnight.

- To make the sauce, heat the cream and syrup in a medium saucepan over medium-high heat. Once it starts to simmer, remove from the heat and add the chocolate. Let sit for a few minutes, then stir until smooth.

- Cut the cheesecake into wedges and drizzle the warm (not hot) chocolate sauce over top as you serve it.

Serves 12

HOW TO SET A TABLE FOR DINNER GUESTS

Table setting isn't nearly as complicated as it might seem, and knowing a few basic rules will set you up for success no matter what type of meal you're serving.

Decades ago, a standard dinner party was a multicourse formal affair, where guests were gussied up in their Sunday best, the table was properly set with an arsenal of cutlery for the many dishes that made their way onto the table, and the presentation of the meal was almost more important than the taste. While certainly fun at time, this style of entertaining has mostly given way to more casual, intimate gatherings, where guests serve themselves family style, the dress code is a little more relaxed, and those invited are comfortable pouring themselves wine at the table.

Nonetheless, it is important to have a few table-setting basics tucked away for the special occasions that require them. For starters, forks are always set to the left of the plate, with knives and spoons set to the right. If you are serving multiple courses and require more than one fork, place forks on the table in the order that they will be used. The blades of a knife should always face inward, and a napkin always goes to the left of a fork, under the fork or on the centre of the plate. A basic table setting might also include a bread and butter plate, but that's completely optional. If you chose to include them on your table, place them to the left of the plate, over the forks. All drinking glasses—most table settings include water and wine—should be set to the right of the plate, above the knives. Spoons should rest to the right of the knives in the order that they will be used. Meaning, if you are including both a soup spoon and a teaspoon or dessert spoon, the soup spoon will be on the outside of the utensils, and the teaspoon will be nestled between the outside spoon and the nearest knife.

Most of us are unlikely to prepare any kind of dinner that demands more knowledge than this. If a meal requires specialty serving items or more than two of any one specific utensil, it's probably destined for a more formal setting. Strive to keep things as simple as possible and if a flow chart is required to keep the tableware organized, chances are you may not have planned the perfect dinner for your guests.

When it comes to serving pieces, a basic collection of plates, bowls and side plates are nice to have on hand. If possible, this may also include a reasonably-sized collection of serving platters and bowls. Glass or white coloured items work well because they match almost any special occasion and can be jazzed up with colourful linens and simple table décor that suits the season. If your serving accessories don't match, don't fret; a contrasting collection of items can add charm to any table. Lastly, consider investing in a quality wooden cutting board. While essential to the process of preparing a dinner, this classic kitchen item also has many uses when entertaining your guests. It can easily double as a serving board for cheeses or other nibbles, and it works well as a serving board for home-made pizzas. Furthermore, a cutting board is indispensable when it comes to carving beef, ham or lamb at the table or on a buffet.

DATE *Night* (OR DINNER FOR TWO)

SOME OF MY best-loved gatherings have been the ones that included just a small handful of people. Smaller groups are more intimate, with the conversations easier to keep track of, and while I always eagerly anticipate hosting a large crowd, spending an evening with just a few friends can be equally as rewarding. A gathering is no less significant if there are two people at the table instead of ten. In fact, when I think about an average family dinner or at-home date night, those get-togethers will be some of the most important "gatherings" I experience in my lifetime, I'm sure of it. Naturally, I'll always remember our big summer barbecues, holiday dinners with extended family, and birthday bashes, but an intimate dinner for two, whether eaten by candlelight or on the couch in front of the TV, will stay with me far longer.

My husband Rob and I have a long-standing tradition of weekly date nights at home. The structure and set-up has shifted over the years, morphing into something different each season as we take into consideration our growing children, work commitments and general responsibilities, but the effort to maintain this ritual has turned our ordinary, happy marriage into one with a splash of spiciness and extra fun.

We officially started these dinners for two when our boys were toddlers, born less than two years apart from one another. We set out with a goal to "keep the romance" alive amid the happy chaos that accompanied new parenthood and "two under two." While our initial intentions were simply to have peaceful dinners free from interruption and cartoon character place settings, we quickly realized that we could add movies, board games and great conversation to our meals, replicating the great nights out that we cherished but had recently found difficult to organize. We chose Wednesday nights because they gave us something special to look forward to, adding an extra dose of fun to a regular weeknight.

The menu in this chapter isn't created specifically for a date, although it does lend itself well to a romantic repast for two, and would certainly make a nice meal option for a Valentine's Day dinner at home. However, I also like the idea of using it as the basis for inviting a close friend over and serving them food made in your own kitchen instead of going out to eat at a local restaurant. It's more relaxing, fun, cost-effective and possibly even interactive, if you choose to make the cooking part of your evening a project you work on together. Take note—while we've labeled this menu as a meal for two, don't hesitate to make any of these recipes just for yourself, keeping the leftovers tucked away for another meal on a different day.—JS

PEAR, AVOCADO AND ROQUEFORT SALAD

This salad for two is very generous in its serving size and would be perfect on it's own with some crusty bread and chilled white wine. Should you choose to serve it with the Mussels with Garlic, Lemon and Tomato (page 233) or the Simple French Onion Soup (page 230) you may end up with leftovers, or alternatively you can halve the ingredient list, making the portion sizes smaller.

2 Tbsp (30 mL) pure maple syrup

½ cup (125 mL) pecans

½ head butter lettuce, leaves torn

1 head Belgian endive, ends trimmed, core removed and leaves separated

1 pear, cored and thinly sliced

1 avocado, peeled, pitted and diced

¼ cup (60 mL) thinly sliced red onion

¼ cup (60 mL) dried cranberries

3 oz (90 g) Roquefort cheese, crumbled

Honey Mustard Vinaigrette (page 229)

- In a skillet set over medium heat, stir the maple syrup and pecans together. Continue stirring gently until the syrup is reduced and the pecans are caramelized. Spoon nuts onto a piece of parchment and allow to cool. Break into pieces if needed and set aside.

- In a serving bowl, layer the lettuce with the endive, pear, avocado and red onion. Sprinkle the dried cranberries over and cover with the crumbled Roquefort. Drizzle the vinaigrette on the salad and scatter the pecans over the top.

Makes 2 generous portions

HONEY MUSTARD VINAIGRETTE

6 Tbsp (90 mL) olive or safflower oil

2 Tbsp (30 mL) lemon juice

1 tsp (5 mL) Dijon mustard

2 tsp (10 mL) honey

1 garlic clove, minced

¼ tsp (1 mL) salt

- Place all of the ingredients in a jam jar. Fasten the lid and shake well to combine. Store in the fridge for up to 3 days.

PARTY POINTER This dressing tastes best when the flavours have had some time to mingle in the jar. If possible, make it at least one day before you need it. Use the best oil and vinegar you can afford; it really does make a difference in the flavour of the dressing.

Makes ½ cup (125 mL)

SIMPLE FRENCH ONION SOUP

French onion soup sounds fancy, but in reality it's one of the easiest soups you can whip up, using ingredients you likely already have on hand. Be sure to use a variety of wine that you enjoy drinking—you'll have a good portion of the bottle leftover to drink with the soup.

1 Tbsp (15 mL) butter

1 Tbsp (15 mL) olive oil

2 medium Spanish onions, thinly sliced

1 bay leaf

1 sprig thyme

1 tsp (5 mL) kosher salt

1 tsp (5 mL) sugar

½ cup (125 mL) red wine

1 Tbsp (15 mL) all-purpose flour

2 cups (500 mL) beef stock

salt and pepper

two–four 1-inch (2.5 cm) thick slices of baguette, toasted

2 oz (60 g) aged cheddar or Gruyere cheese, grated

· Melt the butter and olive oil in a stockpot set over medium-high heat. Add the onions, bay leaf, thyme, salt and sugar, and cook, stirring occasionally, for 10 minutes or until the onions begin to soften and colour. Reduce the heat to medium and cook for an additional 10–15 minutes, or until the onions are very caramelized.

· Discard the bay leaf and stems from the thyme; pour in the wine, scraping the bottom of the pot as you stir to lift the browned bits from the bottom. Sprinkle the flour over the onions and stir to combine. Cook for 2 minutes.

· Add the beef stock and bring the soup back up to a boil. Reduce heat and simmer for an additional 10 minutes. Taste and season the soup with salt and pepper, if necessary.

· Preheat the broiler. Divide the soup evenly between two oven-safe bowls. Top each serving with a piece or two of bread and half of the grated cheese. Transfer bowls to a rimmed baking sheet and place in the oven. Cook until the cheese is golden brown and bubbly, about 2 minutes.

Serves 2

MUSSELS WITH GARLIC, TOMATO AND LEMON

If you like, add a splash of white wine to the pan, then cook until it has almost evaporated before adding the tomato and mussels. This recipe can easily be doubled to feed more.

1 Tbsp (15 mL) butter

1 Tbsp (15 mL) olive or canola oil

¼ cup (60 mL) finely chopped purple onion

2 garlic cloves, crushed or finely chopped

1 Roma tomato, finely chopped

juice of half a lemon

1 lb (500 g) fresh mussels, scrubbed (discard any that are already open)

¼–½ cup (60–125 mL) heavy cream or half & half

chopped fresh Italian parsley or basil, for garnish

- In a large, heavy saucepan, heat the butter and oil over medium-high heat. Add the onion and cook for 3–4 minutes, until soft. Add the garlic and cook for another minute.

- Add the tomato, lemon juice, mussels and cream; cover and simmer for 5 minutes, until the mussels have opened. (Discard any that don't open.)

- Divide between 2 wide, shallow bowls; scatter with chopped parsley and serve immediately with crusty bread and an empty bowl for discarding shells.

PARTY POINTER This will serve 4 as an appetizer and makes a tasty first course for most dinner parties

Serves 2

NO-BAKE CHOCOLATE POTS
DE CRÈME WITH ORANGE WHIPPED CREAM

Bypassing the traditional method of baking with a water bath, this quick, no-bake version of a French pot de crème delivers a rich chocolate confection that is smooth like a pudding, yet simultaneously airy and fluffy and reminiscent of a traditional mousse. I like to serve the little cups with a crisp cookie on the side of the plate, offering a little crunch for the dish, but if you choose to serve them just as they are you certainly won't be disappointed.

POT DE CRÈME

1 cup (250 mL) good quality semi-sweet chocolate chips

2 tsp (10 mL) sugar

1 egg, at room temperature

1 tsp (5 mL) vanilla

pinch salt

1 cup (250 mL) heavy (whipping) cream, chilled

ORANGE WHIPPED CREAM

½ cup (125 mL) heavy (whipping) cream, chilled

1 tsp (5 mL) orange liqueur or orange juice

2 tsp (10 mL) sugar

½ tsp (2.5 mL) finely grated orange zest, for garnish

- Place the chocolate chips and sugar in the bowl of a food processor fitted with a steel blade and pulse until ground. Add the egg, vanilla and salt, and blend until smooth, about 1 minute.

- Meanwhile, heat the cream in a saucepan set over medium heat, until steam rises and bubbles begin to form around the perimeter of the pot.

- Scrape down the bowl of the food processor. Turn the motor on and slowly drizzle the hot cream into the machine. Blend for 1 minute or until smooth and the chocolate is completely melted.

- Divide the mixture into two coffee cups, ramekins or small jars. Cover with plastic wrap and chill for a minimum of 2–4 hours or overnight.

- To make the whipped cream, beat the whipping cream, orange liqueur and sugar in a medium bowl until peaks form. This can be done up to 2 hours in advance. Chill.

- Uncover the pots de crèmes and spoon a dollop of whipped cream topping over each. Garnish with the orange zest, dividing it evenly between the cups and serve.

PARTY POINTER This recipe can easily be doubled or tripled to serve a crowd.

Makes 2 large or 4 small portions

COCKTAIL *Party*

THROWING A COCKTAIL party sounds like a fussy and fancy way to entertain, but in reality hosting one is a classic method of sharing food and drink with friends and business associates casually and without a huge investment of time. Typical cocktail parties last two to three hours, and guests snack on simple, easy-to-eat finger foods while sipping on cocktails. Generally more of a stand up affair (as those invited walk around and chat rather than staying stationary in a seat), this style of party also works well for an open house or a pre-dinner gathering.

When it comes to the food, keep in mind that your friends need to be able to juggle their drinks and edibles without worrying about melted cheeses running down the front of their fancy party clothes. Put your focus on making self-contained items that can be eaten in one to three bites, while taking care to avoid drippy sauces and other messy items. With respect to drinks, I like to keep it simple by offering guests a choice of one red wine, one white wine, beer and a cocktail (or a fun welcome drink) that represents the season or special occasion—if it can be made and served in a pitcher or punch bowl, even better).

There are a few things to consider as you begin the planning process for this type of soiree, which can really be as simple or complex as you like, depending on what you decide to offer. Here is a small list of questions to ask yourself as you sit down and put pen to paper:

- How many guests are you inviting?
- What is your budget?
- Are you serving a full bar or a wine/beer bar?

- What is the timing of your cocktail party? If the gathering is planned for a time in which you would normally eat a meal, you will need to offer more food than usual (see How to Feed a Crowd, page 174).
- Is the party indoors or outdoors?
- Is there a theme for the party?
- Will you hire someone to help serve the food and drinks, or to watch over the kids?
- Do you require rentals of glassware or other small items?

Ice supply is almost always overlooked when it comes to planning drinks, but it's an essential part of their success. Estimate one pound of ice per person; it may seem like a lot, but you want to fill glasses with as many cubes as possible, keeping the drinks well chilled. You will also need ice for chilling bottles of wine and beer (you can do this in a cooler outside if you don't have a large ice tub or space in your fridge) and keep in mind that if you're hosting an outdoor party during the warm summer months, you'll lose a good amount of ice due to melting. If your fridge isn't equipped with an ice machine, purchase bags at the grocery store or gas station, or order it with other rentals you may have secured, as most party supply rental companies offer ice in 40-50 lb (18-22.5 kg) bags.—JS

15 EASY NO-COOK FOODS TO SERVE WITH DRINKS

While Julie and I are obviously both passionate about cooking, we also happen to believe that good food can just as easily be assembled without too much time spent standing by the stove. A quick trip to a well-stocked supermarket can yield a delicious assortment of nutritious nibbles that go from package to plate in no time. Fill a selection of small bowls and platters full of any of the below items, and place them within easy reach of your guests; no one will leave hungry or disappointed.

- Salted nuts, like Marcona almonds or roasted pistachios.

- Bowls of clementines, cherries or Concord grapes—whatever's in season.

- Store-bought cheese straws.

- Spicy salami, cherry tomatoes and crisp cucumber.

- Store-bought hummus topped with a drizzle of olive oil and a sprinkling of smoked paprika, with fresh crudité or torn pita bread.

- Thin slices of pear wrapped with a slice of prosciutto.

- Deli-sliced roast beef on rye bread spread with mustard. Top with cornichon, if desired.

- Marinated olives, sliced feta and spiced flatbread.

- Smoked salmon on cream cheese-topped mini bagels with finely sliced red onion and capers.

- Halved figs topped with creamy ricotta, a drizzle of golden honey and crushed pistachios.

- Round tortilla chips topped with a dollop of store-bought salsa, a dribble of sour cream, grated cheddar or Monterey Jack and fresh cilantro.

- Potato chips or silver dollar pancakes topped with crème fraîche and thin slices of smoked salmon or caviar.

- Endive leaves with fig jam, pear slices, crumbled blue cheese and candied walnuts.

- Pâté, cornichons and fresh or toasted baguettes.

- Baby bocconcini tossed with olive oil, red pepper flakes and fresh herbs—or bottled pesto—with crisp crackers.

PARMESAN AND THYME PUFFS

Perfect for parties, these cheesy puffs are one of my favourite nibbles and for good reason: they're easy to assemble and a crowd-pleasing favourite, leaving guests happy and satiated. I like to stuff these savoury snacks with bits of ham or tuna salad, and during the winter holidays they taste fabulous when filled with turkey and a thick smear of cranberry sauce.

½ cup (125 mL) milk

½ cup (125 mL) water

6 Tbsp (90 mL) butter

½ tsp (2.5 mL) salt

1 cup (250 mL) all-purpose flour

4 large eggs

1¼ cups (310 mL) grated Parmesan cheese

zest of 1 lemon

2 tsp (10 mL) fresh thyme leaves, plus extra for garnish

1 egg, beaten with 1 Tbsp (15 mL) water

- Preheat the oven to 400°F (200°C), and line 2 baking sheets with parchment paper.

- Combine the milk, water, butter and salt in a saucepan set over medium heat and cook until the butter melts and the liquid starts to boil. Immediately add the flour and stir until a dough ball forms and pulls away from the sides of the pot. Continue stirring vigorously until the dough is no longer sticky and a film forms on the bottom of the pan.

- Stir enthusiastically for another minute or so, until the dough is smooth and glossy. This is important because if the batter is too loose when you begin incorporating the eggs, the dough will not puff properly come baking time.

- Transfer to the bowl of a food processor or electric mixer and allow the dough to cool for 5 minutes. Add the eggs, one a time, fully incorporating each one before adding the next. Scrape down the bowl each time and check the consistency of the paste. It should be stiff enough to stand, but soft enough to spread. Add the Parmesan, lemon zest and thyme leaves and pulse just until combined.

- Using an ice cream scoop, 2 spoons or a piping bag fitted with a wide round tip, drop tablespoon-sized dollops of the paste onto prepared baking sheets. Using damp fingers, press down any irregularities in the shape, forming a small smooth ball. Brush the tops of the dough with the egg wash mixture and sprinkle the extra thyme leaves over top of each pastry puff.

- Bake for 20–25 minutes, or until the cheese puffs are golden, dry and firm to the touch.

PARTY POINTER Puffs can be piped and frozen individually on a baking sheet before being stored collectively in freezer bags for up to 2 months. If you choose to make them in advance, don't brush the egg wash over top or add the extra thyme leaves until just before baking. You can also bake them up to 3 hours in advance and then reheat in a 350°F (175°C) oven for 3–5 minutes just before serving. Lastly, the dough can be piped, baked, cooled, frozen and stored in a freezer-friendly container. To reheat, warm puffs in a 350°F (175°C) oven until hot.

BACON-WRAPPED DATES WITH PARMESAN

This is another recipe that gets called into service often. Meaty Medjool dates are usually found in the produce section of the supermarket, rather than the baking aisle; pull their pits out and replace them with a chunk of cheese, wrap in a piece of bacon and bake until the bacon is cooked and the cheese is melted. That's it. You'll be lucky if you make it out of the kitchen with a batch. They can be prepped in advance and lie in wait in the fridge until you're ready to slide them into the oven for about 10 minutes. Multiply ingredients to make as many as you'd like.

18 Medjool dates

eighteen 1-inch (2 cm) thick chunks Parmesan or Asiago cheese

9 slices bacon or prosciutto

- Preheat the oven to 400°F (200°C). Pull the pits out of the dates and push a piece of Parmesan into each. Cut bacon slices in half crosswise (or prosciutto in half lengthwise) and wrap a piece around each stuffed date.

- Place seam side down on a rimmed baking sheet and bake for 10 minutes, or until the bacon is cooked and cheese is oozing out the middle. Serve warm.

PARTY POINTER Feel free to replace the Parmesan with blue cheese for a unique twist on this popular party snack.

Serves a small crowd

MINI PAVLOVA WITH LEMON CURD

Mini pavlovas (meringue nests) are a classy alternative to the usual finger sweets (cookies, squares) at a party; they call for six egg whites, meaning you'll have six yolks with which to make lemon curd to fill them with. Top with fresh berries, pomegranate arils or any fruit in season. The meringues can be made ahead and stored in an airtight container for up to a week; fill them just before serving.

MERINGUES

1½ cups (375 mL) sugar

1½ tsp (7.5 mL) cornstarch

6 large egg whites

½ tsp (2.5 mL) white vinegar

½ tsp (2.5 mL) vanilla

Lemon Curd (page 247)

fresh berries or pomegranate arils

whipped cream

- Preheat the oven to 250°F (120°C) and line 2 large baking sheets with foil or parchment.

- Stir together the sugar and cornstarch. In a large, clean glass or stainless steel bowl, beat the egg whites with an electric mixer until soft peaks form. Gradually add the sugar a bit at a time, beating constantly until the mixture holds stiff, glossy peaks, and has the consistency of shaving cream. Beat in the vinegar and vanilla.

- Spoon small mounds of meringue about 1 inch (2.5 cm) apart on the lined baking sheets, then make little indents in the middle using the tip of a teaspoon, forming nests. Bake one sheet at a time (or both in a convection oven) for 1 hour each, until crisp and dry. Let the meringues cool completely, then peel them off the foil or parchment.

- Right before serving, fill each pavlova with a small spoonful of lemon curd and/or whipped cream, then top with berries or chopped fresh fruit.

Makes about 40 pavlovas

LEMON CURD

6 egg yolks

1 cup (250 mL) sugar

½ cup (125 mL) lemon juice

zest of 1 or 2 lemons

⅓ cup (80 mL) butter, cut into pieces

· In a medium saucepan, whisk together the egg yolks, sugar, lemon juice and zest. Set over medium heat and cook, stirring constantly, until the mixture comes to a boil and thickens.

· Remove from the heat and stir in the butter. Set aside for a few minutes, until the butter melts, then whisk until smooth and refrigerate until well chilled.

PARTY POINTER Lemon curd is the perfect companion to meringue (which leaves you with exactly enough egg yolk for this recipe!), and it keeps well, so you can make both ahead of time and assemble them right before serving. Lemon curd is also delicious to have on hand at a tea party or brunch when there are scones on the table.

Makes about 2 cups (500 mL)

CROSTINI

Part of my personal entertaining strategy is to ensure that all my gatherings are simple affairs that make my guests feel comfortable and well fed, while simultaneously keeping me a relaxed and happy hostess. This encompasses everything from table décor to beverages, but most importantly it extends to food. As such, I'm always on the look out for easy-to-execute, lip-smacking appetizers that deliver impressive tastes. Luckily, crostini fits the bill perfectly.

The name sounds highly impressive (they are also known as tartines) but really these basic bites are actually nothing more than thin slices of toasted or grilled bread garnished with a little something. It can be as simple as a thick slathering of mustard topped with aged cheddar or assorted spreads like hummus and tzatziki, or it can incorporate cured meats or fresh produce that's paired with fresh, fragrant herbs and a variety of oils.

1 long baguette, sliced into ½-inch (1 cm) thick pieces

½ cup (125 mL) olive oil

salt and pepper

· Brush both sides of the bread with olive oil and season the top with a gentle sprinkling of salt and pepper.

· Toast on a grill or in a pre-heated oven at 350°F (175°C) for 15–20 minutes, until browned and crisp. Add the desired toppings, and serve.

PARTY POINTER More often than not, you don't require an actual recipe for these easy appetizers. Once the bread is prepared you can let your imagination run wild as you cover your toast with anything on hand. For extra fun, consider setting up a DIY crostini bar complete with baskets of prepared bread and platters of cheeses, meats, spreads, fresh produce, herbs, olive oil, sea salt, etc. Allowing your guests to create their own custom flavours is a fun and fuss-free way to entertain, and who knows, you just might end up with a new favourite flavour combination to tuck into your back-pocket for the next time you're on the look out for an easy appetizer.

15 WAYS TO TOP YOUR CROSTINI

Raiding your pantry, fridge and garden for a few favourite ingredients is sure to yield delicious results, but if you're looking for a little extra inspiration here are some crostini combinations that are worth trying:

- avocado, lime juice, sea salt, red pepper flakes
- sweet butter, radish slices, sea salt
- shrimp, mayonnaise, tarragon
- ricotta cheese, roasted tomato, chopped basil
- blue cheese, fig, honey
- goat cheese, roasted garlic, fresh thyme
- tuna salad, black olive, lemon zest
- sweet pea, Parmesan, mint
- pear, pecans, Stilton
- apple, walnut, Roquefort
- goat cheese, roasted grapes, fresh thyme
- white bean puree, sundried tomatoes, rosemary
- Brie, cranberry sauce, sage leaf
- Burrata, strawberry jam, basil
- grilled corn, feta, cilantro, lime
- whipped feta, cherry tomato, pine nuts

PROSCIUTTO PRAWNS WITH PESTO

This simple recipe is great to have in your back pocket for any party that requires a nibble; prawns are wrapped in prosciutto and quickly cooked in a skillet, then served with pesto. One of the simplest finger foods just happens to be one of the most delicious.

1 lb (500 g) raw peeled, tail-on shrimp

12 or so thin slices of prosciutto

olive or canola oil, for cooking

bottled pesto, for serving

- Pat the shrimp dry with paper towels. Cut each piece of prosciutto in half lengthwise and wrap one piece around each shrimp; it's tacky enough to keep closed without the need for a toothpick. Wrap all the shrimp in prosciutto and set aside.

- In a large, heavy skillet, heat a drizzle of oil over medium-high heat. Cook the prawns without crowding the pan, turning as needed until the shrimp turn opaque. Transfer to a serving platter as they're done; overcooking will result in tough shrimp.

- Serve immediately, with a small dish of pesto for dipping.

Serves 10

THE FRENCH 75

Named after a rifle that was said to have the same kick as this cocktail, the first French 75, a sophisticated yet simple drink, was made in 1915 at Harry's New York Bar in Paris, France. It was popularized in North America by soldiers returning from the First World War, and is easily one of the best tasting cocktails you can serve at any party.

1 oz (30 mL) gin

½ oz (15 mL) simple syrup

½ oz (15 mL) lemon juice

Prosecco or sparkling wine

ice

lemon slice or twist

· Combine gin, simple syrup and lemon juice in a cocktail shaker filled with ice and shake vigorously. Strain into a champagne glass and top with Prosecco. Garnish with lemon slice or twist.

PARTY POINTER You can make this same drink using vodka instead of gin, which is known as a French 76.

Serves 1

HOW TO BUILD A CHEESE BOARD

With such a wide variety of cheeses available, a cheese board is a convenient way to feed people, whether they're coming over or you've been asked to bring something to a party. Cheese is perfect for all ages, and a board or platter can be made bigger or smaller depending on how many guests you have to feed. Plan on serving about 2 oz (60 g) of cheese per guest, assuming there are going to be other nibbles available at the party. (Leftover cheese is never a problem.)

However big or small your cheese board, include a variety of cheeses—no fewer than three and no more than eight—all with different flavours and textures. Start with either a wood cutting board, a long platter, a framed mirror (this is a trick many caterers use) or even a slate kitchen tile from Home Depot (I often put peel and stick rubber or felt bumpers on the bottom to make it easier to lift and protect the table), which stays cool and looks great with cheese and its accessories. Go for one universally friendly cheese, like aged cheddar or Gouda, and a goat's milk option in case anyone can't tolerate dairy. A blue cheese adds contrast, as does a runny Brie.

When setting out your board, avoid pre-cutting the cheeses—cubing or slicing creates more surface area, making the cheeses dry out quickly. Simply take your cheeses out of the fridge (they will have better flavour at room temperature than when they're refrigerator-cold) and place the larger pieces before the smaller ones.

Beyond that, almost anything goes. Interesting crackers, dense breads (such as Irish soda, nut and olive loaves) and baguettes are all great accompaniments, as are small bunches of grapes to nestle among the cheeses for something juicy and acidic. Tuck in wee bowls or pots of preserves, chutney or olive tapenade along with dried apricots, figs and whole nuts (such as walnuts, pecans and almonds) for a sweet and crunchy contrast to the soft cheese you can tuk in the empty spaces. Add a couple small knives, and replenish the smaller bits as necessary.

See? It's easy being cheesy.

STOCKING THE BAR
AND PURCHASING ALCOHOL

The following lists can serve as a guideline for how much alcohol you might need to purchase when entertaining. While I'm not personally a fan of serving a full bar, some events do require it, and the chart below includes lists of what you will require per person if you choose to go this route.

A FEW BASIC THINGS TO REMEMBER

- A standard serving of wine is 5 oz (150 mL) so a 750 mL bottle will yield 5 drinks, a 1 L bottle will give 7 and a 1.5 L bottle will provide 10 drinks.

- A 750 mL bottle of liquor will provide 17 ordinary drinks. For mix you will need three similar-sized bottles. The most common liquors to purchase are, in order: vodka, rum, Canadian whisky/rye, scotch/bourbon, gin and brandy.

- Generally, one bottle of beer is equal to one serving, i.e. a case of 24 beers is equal to 24 servings of alcohol.

FOR A FULL BAR (BASED ON ANY NUMBER OF GUESTS)

- ½–⅔ bottle of wine per person

- 1½ bottles of beer per person

- 4 cups (1 L) of sparkling water per 4 guests

- ½ can soda/mix per person (diet cola, cola, ginger ale, tonic, soda water)

- 2 oz (60 mL) vodka, rum, Canadian whisky/rye per person

- 1 oz (30 mL) scotch/bourbon, gin and brandy per person

- Lemons and limes

- Large green olives

- Optional: juices, mineral water, specialty cocktail items

- ½–⅔ bottle of wine per person

- 1½ bottles of beer per person

- 4 cups (1 L) of sparkling water per 4 guests

- Lemons and limes

- Optional: juices, mineral water, specialty cocktail items

BAR SUPPLIES (BASED ON ANY NUMBER OF GUESTS)

- 1 lb (500 g) ice per person for chilling and drinking

- Cocktail napkins

- 1–2 glasses per person

- Wine opener

- Optional: ice bucket and scoop, ice tub or cooler for chilling, tongs, shot glass, muddler, swizzle sticks, specialty glassware, cocktail shaker, paring knife, garnish (pomegranate seeds, lemon twists, orange slices, etc.)

PARTY POINTER To keep your party simple, offer wine and beer plus one signature drink. Ideally, serve something that can be premade in a pitcher, leaving out any fizzy ingredients and adding them just before serving.

BOOK Club

Taking part in a book club is something I really adore. An evening gathered with like-minded friends, chatting about books and, in our case, food, is a pretty perfect way to spend time with people I really like as far as I'm concerned.

Book clubs have been around since the mid-15th century, when the first printing press was invented. By the 18th and 19th centuries, Parisian literary groups (called "salons") were at the centre of cerebral learning in Europe, and women often hosted intellectual gatherings to discuss books and philosophy and their criticisms of both. The atmosphere of these intimate meetings was casual and even known to take place in the boudoir, with guests seated on the floor while the hostess remained in bed for the discussion. Obviously, book clubs are a little different today, and while inviting friends to your home to discuss something you've mutually read is still a popular practice, online clubs are also popping up, allowing literary discussions to take place on blogs and social media websites. I haven't attempted a web-based book club yet, and I'm quite confident I won't be discussing the latest bestseller while tucked between the sheets of my bed, but I am definitely on board with the idea of gathering in person to discuss the merits, or failings, of a book we've all read.

Of course it goes without saying that there must also be munchies at these gatherings, and I'm inclined to think that these items should be easy to eat and prepare. Garlic bread focaccia, maple caramel corn and hoisin pork lettuce wraps are do-ahead options that are always popular with a crowd. For a sweet finish to the evening I like to put out a plate of bourbon blondies, spiked with chocolate and nuts and served alongside coffee or tea, which almost always signals it's time to wrap up the discussion.—JS

HOW TO START A BOOK CLUB

- Decide on the purpose of your book club and how many members you'd like to have.

- Ask your friends what kinds of books they enjoy and request that each member come to the first meeting with 2–3 suggestions for what to read. Encourage them to bring reviews or online ratings for their book, as well as an explanation of what appeals to them about their recommended titles.

- Determine a meeting place, be it a coffee shop, someone's home or the library, and schedule your meetings. If you organize the book club and host the first meeting, you are not required to host the remainder of the meetings. However, it's also not imperative that every person in the group take a turn hosting, either. If it doesn't work with a member's schedule or lifestyle, they can contribute to the book club in other ways, like bringing food to each meeting or overseeing the administrative duties (such as tracking which books have been read, which are on the "to read" list, etc.)

- Important things to discuss before the first meeting: Who will lead the first meeting? Who will lead subsequent meetings—the person who suggested the book, or the host of the meeting? Will refreshments be served? Will the host take care of the food, or will the meeting follow a potluck format?

- Encourage the leader of the discussion to come to the club with prepared questions in mind. These can be found at the back of some books and on the websites of many authors or publishers.

HOW TO HOST A COOKBOOK CLUB

If you love food as much as I do, you might want to consider starting a cookbook club. I've created one with a few of my friends, and instead of tearing our way through the pages of bestselling novels or self-help tomes, we read cookbooks, and cook from them for our book club meetings. We've kept our group small and currently only boast three members, meaning each of us can take charge of one of the courses we've divided our meal into: appetizer, main and dessert. The person hosting is in charge of the primary dish because it's easier for them to cook and serve something hot. The other two bring snacks for the cocktail hour and dessert for the end of the meal, and we all share a meal while discussing the book we cooked from.

RECOMMENDED FOOD LITERATURE FOR BOOK CLUBS

- *Tender at the Bone* by Ruth Reichl
- *Comfort Me with Apples* by Ruth Reichl
- *Home Cooking* by Laurie Colwin
- *A Homemade Life* by Molly Wizenberg
- *Dinner: A Love Story* by Jenny Rosenstrach
- *Animal, Vegetable, Mineral* by Barbara Kingsolver
- *Bread and Wine* by Shauna Niequist
- *Blood, Bones & Butter* by Gabrielle Hamilton
- *Heartburn* by Nora Ephron
- *Cooking for Mr. Latte* by Amanda Hesser
- *The Sharper Your Knife, The Less You Cry* by Kathleen Flinn
- *The Cook and the Gardener* by Amanda Hesser
- *An Everlasting Meal* by Tamar Adler
- *My Berlin Kitchen* by Luisa Weiss
- *Alice, Let's Eat* by Calvin Trillin
- *The Language of Baklava* by Diana Abu-Jaber
- *Lunch in Paris: A Love Story with Recipes* by Elizabeth Bard
- *My Life from Scratch* by Gesine Bullock-Prado
- *The Feast Nearby* by Robin Mather

GARLIC BREAD FOCACCIA

A simple, comforting garlicky focaccia is easy to make and serve; cut into squares and offer a dish of olive oil and balsamic vinegar, for dipping.

GARLIC OIL

¼ cup (60 mL) olive oil

3 garlic cloves

¼ cup (60 mL) chopped fresh parsley, divided

1 tsp (5 mL) kosher salt

½ tsp (2.5 mL) freshly ground black pepper

DOUGH

1 cup (250 mL) warm water

1 Tbsp (15 mL) honey

2 tsp (10 mL) active dry yeast

3¼ cups (810 mL) all-purpose flour

1 tsp (5 mL) kosher salt

3 Tbsp (45 mL) garlic oil (above)

olive oil

1–2 Tbsp (15–30 mL) cornmeal

¼ cup (60 mL) grated Parmesan cheese

- To make the garlic oil, combine the olive oil, garlic, 2 Tbsp (30 mL) of the parsley leaves and the salt and pepper in the bowl of a food processor fitted with a steel blade, pulsing until the garlic and parsley are minced. Alternatively, you can chop the garlic and parsley by hand and combine in a small bowl with the olive oil, salt and pepper.

- To make the dough, place the water and honey is large bowl. Sprinkle with the yeast and whisk together; let stand until foamy, about 5 minutes.

- Stir in 3 cups (750 mL) of the flour, salt and garlic oil, and mix well. Knead in enough of the remaining flour to create a soft dough that isn't sticky. Knead it for a few minutes more, until smooth and elastic, and transfer to a lightly oiled bowl. Cover with a tea towel or plastic wrap, and let rise in a warm place until doubled in size, about 45 minutes.

- Preheat the oven to 400°F (200°C). Coat a large, rimmed baking sheet with a thin layer of olive oil and lightly sprinkle cornmeal over top. Transfer the dough to the baking pan and shape into a 12-inch (30 cm) circle. Poke holes all over with your fingers to dimple the top. Cover and let rise for an additional 30 minutes, or until doubled in bulk.

- Smear the remaining garlic oil over top and cover with the Parmesan cheese. Bake for 15–17 minutes, or until golden brown; top with the remaining parsley leaves and serve warm or at room temperature.

PARTY POINTER Focaccia dough can be made a day in advance. Let it slowly rise in the fridge covered with plastic wrap for 24 hours.

Serves 6–8

SPICY MAPLE CARAMEL CORN

This a popular party snack for both kids and adults alike, but it also makes a mighty fun homemade gift when attractively packaged in a large Mason jar or cellophane bag. Although uncomplicated to make, it's important to pay attention to the instructions in this recipe, following them as closely as you can.

10 cups (2.5 L) popcorn, popped by any method, lightly salted

1 cup (250 mL) brown sugar

½ cup (125 mL) pure maple syrup or corn syrup

6 Tbsp (90 mL) butter

1 tsp (5 mL) baking soda

1 tsp (5 mL) vanilla

1–2 tsp (5–10 mL) Sriracha or a pinch of cayenne pepper (optional)

1 cup (250 mL) salted peanuts

- Preheat the oven to 250°F (120°C) and line a large rimmed baking sheet with parchment paper. Place the popcorn in a large mixing bowl and set aside.

- In a medium saucepan, combine the brown sugar, maple syrup and butter and bring to a boil over medium heat. Reduce the heat to a simmer and boil without stirring, but swirling the pan occasionally, for 4 minutes. Keep your eyes on the caramel the entire time it's cooking to avoid burning the sugar.

- Remove the syrup from the heat and whisk in the baking soda, vanilla and Sriracha, if using. It will foam up and double in volume, but stir it well to remove any little lumps of baking soda that cling to the caramel.

- Quickly pour the syrup over the popcorn and stir with a heatproof spatula or tongs to coat the popcorn. Add the peanuts and mix well. Scrape the popcorn onto a rimmed baking sheet and bake for 25–30 minutes, stirring halfway through the cooking time. Cool and break apart.

Serves a medium-sized crowd

HOISIN PORK LETTUCE WRAPS

Quick to prepare and fun to eat, it's hard not to love a recipe that encourages your tablemates to make their own meal and eat it with their hands. The preparation of the sticky sweet meat takes less than 20 minutes, and when wrapped in a crisp and cool lettuce blanket the end result is an ideal flavour combination sure to please everyone at the table.

2 Tbsp (30 mL) canola oil

1 small onion, finely chopped

½ cup (125 mL) finely diced red pepper

½ cup (125 mL) finely diced yellow pepper

1 Tbsp (15 mL) grated fresh ginger

1 garlic clove, crushed

1 lb (450 g) ground pork

½ cup (125 mL) hoisin sauce

1 Tbsp (15 mL) sesame seeds

1 green onion, thinly sliced

2 heads Bibb or iceberg lettuce, leaves separated, washed and dried

- Heat the oil in a large skillet set over medium heat. Add the onion, red and yellow peppers and sauté for 1 minute; add the ginger and garlic and cook for an additional minute.

- Crumble the pork into the pan, breaking it up with a wooden spoon as you stir it around the skillet. Cook until the excess moisture evaporates and the meat begins to crisp. Add the hoisin sauce and stir to combine. Reduce the heat to medium low and simmer for 3–5 minutes.

- Transfer the pork to a serving bowl and garnish with the sesame seeds and green onion. Place the bowl on a platter and surround with the lettuce leaves. Encourage everyone to scoop some of the pork mixture into the lettuce leaves to make individual wraps.

PARTY POINTER The meat mixture can be made up to two days in advance and stored in the fridge until ready to serve. To reheat, place meat in a skillet and gently simmer until heated through. Garnish with sesame seeds and sliced green onion before serving.

Serves 6

BOURBON BLONDIES
WITH PECANS AND CHOCOLATE CHUNKS

This intoxicatingly tasty treat is ideal for serving to a crowd of friends. The recipe comes together quickly, and the bourbon pairs perfectly with both chocolate and pecans. Feel free to use one tablespoon less of the booze, if desired, replacing it with extra vanilla extract.

½ cup (125 mL) butter, melted and cooled

1 cup (250 mL) packed brown sugar

1 large egg

2 Tbsp (30 mL) bourbon or whiskey

1 tsp (5 mL) vanilla

1 cup (250 mL) all-purpose flour

½ tsp (2.5 mL) baking powder

¼ tsp (1 mL) salt

½ cup (125 mL) chopped chocolate chunks or chips

½ cup (125 mL) chopped pecans

· Preheat the oven to 350°F (175°C) and butter an 8 × 8-inch (20 × 20 cm) pan. Line it with parchment paper, leaving the excess to hang over the sides. This makes for easy removal and slicing.

· In a medium bowl, stir together the butter and sugar, then add the egg, bourbon and vanilla, mixing until smooth. Add the flour, baking powder and salt and stir until almost combined. Using a rubber spatula stir in the chocolate chunks and pecans and mix until just blended. Scrape the batter into the prepared pan, spreading it evenly with the spatula.

· Bake for 22–25 minutes, or until the edges start to pull away from the sides and the middle is just set. Cool for at least 10 minutes before cutting into squares.

PARTY POINTER These treats travel well and are perfect for potlucks, ski weekends and road trips.

Makes 9–16 blondies

HOW TO BUILD A MEZZE PLATTER

Cheese and charcuterie boards have become all the rage in recent years, but a simple mezze platter (*mezze* refers to small Middle Eastern plates) is just as easy to put together, involving no more than the haphazard arrangement of Mediterranean-inspired cured meats, cheeses, olives, nuts, dips and other nibbles on a board or platter. The combination of savoury items makes a perfect starter to a meal, but can also function as the main attraction at a small get together.

Much of what you'd find on a mezze platter can be picked up at the deli; olives, marinated calamari, stuffed peppers and grape leaves, cured sausages and salamis, chunks of pâté, sundried tomatoes, blocks of feta and tubs of hummus. As with a cheese board, place the large items first, then add smaller ones, folding slices of meat in half or tucking them into little bundles and arranging crackers, breadsticks and fresh or toasted pita wedges in the gaps between the larger items. Don't worry about not having a flair for food arranging—the more rustic it looks, the better. At the end, tuck dried apricots or figs and pistachios into nooks and crannies, keeping extra ingredients in the kitchen for easy replenishing.

PITA CHIPS

To make pita chips, cut pitas into wedges, pull apart the two layers, brush the rough side with oil and sprinkle with salt and pepper or a pinch of dry oregano. Bake at 350 °F (175°C) for 10 minutes, or until golden and crisp.

BEER Tasting

WHETHER OR NOT you want to take the tasting part seriously, there are plenty of gatherings that involve beer. It's as fitting when you're getting together to watch sports as it is for a birthday celebration or even a games night—depending, of course, on who's playing. If beer is your drink of choice and you want to turn it into an actual tasting party, the fact that so many liquor stores now carry a wider assortment of imported stouts and ales makes it simple to pick up a variety of bottles.—JVR

HOW TO HOST A BEER TASTING

A beer tasting party is a great opportunity to try different craft beers from around the world—one bottle can be shared between four to six people, so pick up enough for your guests to sample each one, plus a few extra in case they want to continue tasting after you're done.

- Buy a wide assortment of beers, including a pale ale, IPA, English bitter, Weissbier or Witbier (white beer), dark lager, porter and stout—from a variety of countries.

- Do a bit of research—Google each beer and make a few notes to introduce each one as you pour.

- To chill or not to chill? Some say you can taste beer better at room temperature; try some each way to see if it's true.

- Set out pitchers of water for drinking and rinsing out beer glasses.

- Provide an empty pitcher or vase for people to pour out beers they don't like or don't want to finish.

- Offer plain soda crackers for palate cleansing in between.

- Set out a platter of strong cheeses, pickles and olives to experiment with; guests can see how the taste of salt and brine affects the flavour of various beers.

CLASSIC CHEESE FONDUE

My friend Janice Beaton, a well-known cheese shop owner, once talked me through a homemade cheese fondue, which is something she's been making at JB Fine Cheese and its adjoining restaurant FARM for decades. For a classic approach, Janice recommends Gruyere, Emmenthal and Appenzeller in equal measure, but if you can only find the first two, it will still be delicious. Choose a beer that's not too heavy or hoppy, so that the flavour of the cheese isn't overwhelmed.

1 garlic clove, cut in half

1 lb (500 g) grated Gruyere, Emmenthal and Appenzeller

1 Tbsp (15 mL) cornstarch

1 bottle pale ale

bread cut into cubes

raw or lightly steamed veggies (broccoli, cauliflower, celery, asparagus)

- Rub the inside of a fondue pot with the garlic clove. Toss the grated cheese with the cornstarch in a medium bowl.

- In a heavy saucepan, bring the beer just to a simmer and whisk in the cheese a handful at a time, adding more as each melts. Stir until smooth and pour into the fondue pot. Serve with cubed bread and veggies.

Serves 6

HOMEMADE PRETZELS

Chewy homemade pretzels can come in handy for any type of gathering; if kids are invited, twist them into numbers or letters to suit the occasion. If you like, offer fancy grainy mustards for dipping.

1 Tbsp (15 mL) brown sugar

1 Tbsp (15 mL) active dry yeast

4–5 cups (1–1.25 L) all-purpose flour

2 Tbsp (30 mL) canola or olive oil

1 tsp (5 mL) salt

coarse salt, for sprinkling

grainy mustard, for serving

- Put 1½ cups (375 mL) warm water into a large bowl and sprinkle the sugar and yeast over top; let stand for 5 minutes, until foamy.

- Stir in half the flour, the oil and the salt, and stir until you have a sticky, gummy mixture; add enough of the remaining flour to make a soft, slightly tacky dough. Turn the dough out onto a lightly floured surface and knead, gently incorporating more flour if it sticks to your hands, for 8 minutes, or until the dough is smooth and elastic. Cover with a tea towel and let it rest for about 15 minutes.

- Divide the dough into 10 pieces. Roll each piece into a long, thin rope and shape into a pretzel. Leave them to rise on the countertop for about 20 minutes while you bring a large pot of salted water to a boil. Preheat the oven to 425°F (220°C).

- Reduce the water to a simmer and gently place a few pretzels at a time into the water. Simmer for 1 minute, then flip them over and cook for another 30 seconds. Remove with a slotted spoon and transfer to a parchment-lined baking sheet.

- Sprinkle with salt and bake for 20 minutes, until golden.

Makes about 1½ dozen pretzels

BREAD & BUTTER PICKLES

Whether you're having a cocktail party or just noshing on cheese and charcuterie boards, a jar of pickles set out on the table always seems to be a good fit.

5-6 lb (2.2-2.7 kg) thickly sliced small pickling or tiny English cucumbers

1 red pepper, seeded and sliced

1 small onion, halved and thinly sliced

½ cup (125 mL) coarse pickling salt

3 cups (750 mL) sugar

4 cups (1 L) apple cider vinegar

3 Tbsp (45 mL) pickling spices

- Slice the pickles, red pepper and onion into a large bowl and sprinkle with salt. Toss and refrigerate for about 6 hours. Pour off the excess moisture, rinse and drain well.

- In a large pot, bring the sugar and vinegar to a boil. Add the cucumber mixture and spices and simmer for 1–2 minutes, then divide the pickles into jars and pour over the brine, filling to within half an inch of the rim; wipe the rim clean and seal. Store your pickles in the fridge for a few days before eating, or for up to a month.

Makes about four 1-pint jars

BLACK AND TAN CUPCAKES

A "black and tan" is a classic British beer cocktail made by layering a pale beer with a dark beer. You'd think that beer and sweets don't make a good pairing, but Guinness or other dark stout makes a fantastic chocolate cake, and adds a delicious caramel-like flavour to frosting. If you like, spoon the frosting into a zip-lock baggie, snip off a corner and pipe it out onto the cupcakes.

½ cup (125 mL) butter

1 cup (250 mL) Guinness or other dark stout

1½ cups (375 mL) sugar

¾ cup (185 mL) cocoa

1 cup (250 mL) sour cream

2 large eggs

1 tsp (5 mL) vanilla

2 cups (500 mL) all-purpose flour

2 tsp (10 mL) baking soda

¼ tsp (1 mL) salt

STOUT FROSTING

½ cup (125 mL) butter, at room temperature

3 cups (750 mL) icing sugar

¼–⅓ cup (60–80 mL) Guinness or other dark stout

- Preheat the oven to 350°F (175°C). In a small saucepan, melt the butter with the stout over medium heat; pour into a bowl and whisk in the sugar and cocoa, then the sour cream, eggs and vanilla.

- Stir in the flour, baking soda and salt just until blended. Divide the batter between paper-lined cupcake tins and bake for 25 minutes, or until the tops are springy to the touch.

- In a medium bowl, beat the butter, icing sugar and stout until you have a spreadable frosting; add a little extra beer or sugar if it's too stiff or too soft.

- Let the cupcakes cool completely before spreading or piping with frosting.

Makes about 2 dozen cupcakes

RETRO GAME *Night*

FAMILY GAME NIGHT has become a bit of a tradition in our house, and at least once a month we like to clear the coffee table and settle in for a lazy night at home. Surrounded by colourful playing pieces, classic comfort food and good company, this is one of our preferred ways to spend time in the winter months, and inviting a few friends, neighbours or family members over to join in the fun only makes the night more memorable.

This type of casual gathering isn't just a great way for families to spend a night in, it also happens to work really well for couples in search of a more cost-effective way to socialize, and it's a great alternative to a traditional dinner when you've decided to host an all-ages playdate with another family. It also serves as a creative way to introduce one group of people who might not know each very well—like members of a bridal party—to another, as they'll be forced to interact and chat through game play, which is a wonderful way to break the ice.

While there are plenty of modern board games that work well when playing with a bigger group, I like to make sure I have a few old-fashioned favourites on hand too. Almost everyone knows how to play the games that have filled up our closets and cabinets for decades, and incorporating old favourites keeps me from spending a lot of an evening explaining rules for a new game that may take some time to catch on. Of course, I would never discount the idea of learning to play something new as a group, and if your crowd doesn't mind investing the time it takes to learn the rules, it can be ridiculously fun. So, what do you say? How about scoring points with your kids, spouse, friends, family, girlfriends and even those you don't know all that well by planning a retro games night for an easygoing, but totally fun, evening.—JS

WHAT IF YOU DON'T HAVE ANY BOARD GAMES?

Don't feel compelled to purchase board games straight from the store, as older, much-loved favourites are often easily found at thrift stores and garage sales for less than a quarter of the retail price. Just make sure the game pieces and rules are included, and the playing board is in decent shape. Alternatively, if you don't have a lot of games hanging around, borrow them from a neighbour, or ask your guests to bring their own favourites to increase your options for the evening. A tradition I started with my own boys a few years ago was to buy a new board game for the family every year for Christmas, and then again at the beginning of summer break, allowing us to grow our collection slowly over time. Card games and other pocket or travel games are picked up more frequently throughout the year, and as a result we've amassed quite a collection in just a few years.

STICKY COCKTAIL MEATBALLS

This update on classic 1970s-style sweet and sour meatballs uses orange marmalade in place of the more traditional grape jelly, bringing a much-needed touch of bitterness to an otherwise overly sweet sauce. Chili sauce is a kicked up version of ketchup, usually sold in the same section of the grocery store, but if you can't find it feel free to use ordinary ketchup in its place.

MEATBALLS

½ cup (125 mL) panko or regular breadcrumbs

¼ cup (60 mL) milk

2 lb (1 kg) ground beef

½ cup (125 mL) minced onion

1 clove garlic, minced

1 tsp (5 mL) kosher salt

1 tsp (5 mL) dried oregano

1 Tbsp (15 mL) Worcestershire sauce

1 egg, lightly beaten

canola or vegetable oil, for searing

SAUCE

1 cup (250 mL) chili sauce

1 cup (250 mL) orange marmalade

1 Tbsp (15 mL) soy sauce

pinch red chili flakes

- Preheat the oven to 350°F (175°C).

- In a small bowl combine the panko (or breadcrumbs) and milk; set aside for 3 minutes to allow the crunchy crumbs to soften.

- Place all of the other meatball ingredients into a large mixing bowl. Add the panko mixture and mix well with a fork or your hands; shape into 1-inch (2.5 cm) meatballs.

- In a large skillet set over medium heat, cover the bottom of the pan with oil and cook the meatballs in batches, turning until browned on all sides. Transfer to a paper-towel lined plate to absorb any excess grease.

- Place the meatballs in the bottom of a 2½ quart (2.4 L) casserole or baking dish. Whisk together the sauce ingredients and pour over the meatballs. Bake until the meat is cooked through and the sauce is thick and bubbly, about 20 minutes. Remove from the oven and serve immediately.

PARTY POINTER The sauce can be made up to two days in advance and stored in the refrigerator until needed. Meatballs can also be made two days in advance and stored in the fridge, or up to one month ahead of time and stored in the freezer. To rewarm, place cooked meatballs in a preheated 250°F (120°C) oven and heat until warmed through the centre.

Makes about 5 dozen meatballs

MINI SAUSAGE ROLLS

These popular party bites are so easy to make, you'll never want to purchase store-bought variations again. Equally as good when served hot or at room temperature, they can easily sit out on the table for your friends to graze on. Be sure to serve them with something fun for dipping—I'm partial to assorted mustards, regular or spicy ketchup and a sweet chutney.

1 lb (500 g) pkg good quality mild Italian sausages, casings removed

1 tsp (5 mL) dried oregano

½ tsp (2.5 mL) ground cumin

2 Tbsp (30 mL) grated onion

1 sheet frozen puff pastry, thawed

1 Tbsp (15 mL) Dijon mustard

1 egg, lightly beaten

1 Tbsp (15 mL) sesame seeds

· Preheat the oven to 425°F (220°C) and line a rimmed baking sheet with parchment paper. In a medium bowl combine the sausage meat, dried oregano, ground cumin and grated onion and mix well with a wooden spoon to combine.

· Lightly flour a work surface and roll the puff pastry into a 10 × 13-inch (25 × 33 cm) rectangle. Brush the mustard over the dough and, using a sharp knife or pizza wheel, cut the dough in half lengthwise. Spoon half the sausage mixture down the middle of each piece of pastry, loosely shaping it into a log.

· Fold the long sides of dough over the meat, pressing the edges together and sealing with some of the beaten egg. Cover and freeze until firm, about 20 minutes. Cut each roll into 9 pieces and place them seam side down on the prepared baking sheet, spacing them at least 1 inch (2 cm) apart.

· Brush the remaining beaten egg over the tops of each roll and cover with sesame seeds; bake for 15–20 minutes or until the meat is cooked through and the pastry is golden brown and puffed.

PARTY POINTER To make ahead, proceed as per the recipe directions, returning the rolls to the freezer after they have been cut. Store in an airtight container, keeping layers separated with wax or parchment paper. Brush egg wash over top and garnish with sesame seeds just before placing in the oven. Add an extra 3–5 minutes to the baking time.

Makes 1½ dozen

SOUR CREAM AND BACON DEVILED EGGS

This crowd-pleasing party food never goes out of fashion and is the perfect appetizer for your casual or retro themed parties. This version gets a modern makeover with the addition of sour cream and bacon, and the toasted breadcrumbs add some welcome crunch to a creamy classic.

6 large eggs

2 sliced cooked bacon, finely chopped

¼ cup (60 mL) mayonnaise

¼ cup (60 mL) sour cream

1 tsp (5 mL) Dijon mustard

1 tsp (5 mL) lemon juice

1 green onion, thinly sliced

pinch of cayenne

salt and pepper

1 Tbsp (15 mL) butter

¼ cup (60 mL) panko

- Place the eggs in a single layer in a medium saucepan; add cold water, covering the eggs by at least 1 inch (2.5 cm). Heat on high and bring the water to a boil. Cover, turn off the heat and leave alone for 12 minutes. Drain the hot water from the pot and rinse the cooked eggs under cold water for 1–2 minutes, or until they are cool enough to handle.

- Peel the eggs and, using a sharp knife, slice in half lengthwise. Gently separate the yolks from the whites, placing them in a small mixing bowl. Arrange the whites on a plate or platter and set aside.

- To the mixing bowl add the bacon, mayonnaise, sour cream, Dijon, lemon juice, green onion and cayenne. Mash all of the ingredients together with a fork and season well with salt and pepper.

- Spoon the egg yolk mixture back into the egg white halves, using a spoon or a piping bag fitted with a round or star tip. Place in the fridge while you make the breadcrumb topping.

- Melt the butter in a skillet set over medium heat and add the panko; season with salt and pepper and cook until the breadcrumbs are golden brown. Remove from heat, cool, and sprinkle over eggs just before serving.

PARTY POINTER Feel free to make the filling and breadcrumb topping up to one day in advance. Store the filling in a lidded container in the fridge, and the topping in a lidded container at room temperature; assemble just before serving. If taking these to a potluck, take all of the components separately and assemble the deviled eggs at the party.

Makes 12 deviled eggs

RETRO CHEESE BALL

Who doesn't love a cheese ball? It's the perfect thing to make ahead and keep in the fridge until you need it; roll it around in toasted nuts to coat and you're good to go.

two 8 oz (240 g) pkg cream cheese, at room temperature

2 cups (500 mL) grated old cheddar cheese

1–2 green onions, finely chopped

1 tsp (5 mL) Worcestershire sauce

salt and pepper

1 cup (250 mL) finely chopped toasted pecans or sliced almonds

- In a large bowl, beat the cream cheese until creamy; beat in the cheddar, green onions, Worcestershire sauce and a pinch of salt and pepper. Gather the mixture into a ball and drop it on a square of plastic wrap; wrap the plastic around it and chill for 1 hour, or until firm.

- When ready to serve, place the nuts in a shallow bowl and roll the ball around in them, pressing the nuts to help them adhere until the ball is coated completely. Place on a serving platter and surround with crackers.

Serves 10

CHOCOLATE AND PEANUT BUTTER PUPPY CHOW

Kids and adults will love this tasty gluten-free snack mix. It is guaranteed to disappear the second the bowl hits the table. Any type of Chex works, but corn or rice varieties taste best.

6 cups (1.5 L) Chex cereal

¾ cup (185 mL) icing sugar

¼ cup (60 mL) cocoa

⅔ cup (160 mL) semi-sweet chocolate chips

½ cup (125 mL) peanut butter

2 Tbsp (30 mL) butter

½ tsp (2.5 mL) salt

- Place the cereal in a large bowl. In a small bowl, whisk together the icing sugar and cocoa powder and transfer to a large resealable bag.

- Melt the chocolate chips, peanut butter, butter and salt in the microwave, in 20-second intervals, or in a heatproof bowl set over simmering water, stirring occasionally, until smooth and glossy.

- Immediately pour the mixture over the cereal and stir carefully until the pieces are evenly coated. Scrape the cereal into the resealable bag and seal. Shake gently, until the cereal is well coated with the icing sugar and cocoa mixture.

- Dump the cereal onto a baking sheet and spread into a single layer, letting it cool and dry completely. Can be made up to two days in advance.

Makes 6 cups (1.5 kg)

HOW TO SET UP A CANDY BAR

I fully endorse the idea of setting up a candy bar for a quick and easy snacking station that everyone will love, regardless of their age. Most folks don't consume candy on a regular basis, and assembling small vessels of colourful confections around your space—or grouped together in one central area—will have everyone clamouring for a taste of their favourite sweet treat. It's an easy way to offer quick bites without too much effort, and you can colour coordinate your candy to match any theme, special occasion or holiday, if you choose. While there are no hard and fast rules to assembling a sweets station—it is just candy, after all—it is important to keep these tips in your back pocket when it comes to planning your candy bar.

- Candy isn't only for dessert, so have your jars filled and ready for consumption as soon as your guests arrive.

- Candy can be divided into three categories: bulk candy, individually wrapped candy, and gourmet candy and sweets (like truffles). Estimate approximately 6 oz (175 g) per person of loose candy, and 1½ pieces of the wrapped and specialty candies per person.

- Include tried-and-true (and colourful!) favourites like licorice, jelly beans, jujubes, gummy berries, candy-coated chocolate and lollipops in your selections.

- Use an assortment of containers for your candy; glass vessels work best as they allow you to see what's inside the jar, and it's nice to include a variety of sizes and heights to create visual interest. There's nothing more unsightly than a table full of plates and platters placed at the same height, so try to go vertical with something, whether it's a tiered cake stand, tall glasses of old-fashioned candy sticks or a vase filled with long licorice ropes.

- Truffles and other delicate items should be placed on a platter or cake stand in a single layer. Lollipops can be stored upright and fanned out like straws, and sticky candy like gummy worms can be served from a wide, shallow bowl, in order to keep hands clean.

- Ensure the vessel openings are wide enough for hands to fit through, and use small scoops or tongs to help handle the candy.

- Go for abundance; it's better to see a small urn filled to the brim with candy than a large bowl with a few malt balls inside.

- Label your candies so guests know what they're eating.

- If you don't want to be stuck with sweet leftovers, place a stack of small cellophane bags or Chinese takeout boxes near the candy station and encourage your friends to fill up a doggie bag before they leave.

SLEEPOVER *Party*

A NYONE WITH KIDS will most likely be faced with the prospect of hosting a sleepover at some point; it may not be a party per se, but whether it's a birthday celebration or a regular weekend, it's a gathering of kids who will require feeding—maybe dinner, definitely snacks, probably breakfast.

A large platter of prepared fruit—slices or chunks of melon and pineapple, fresh berries and such—is great to have on hand for nibbling, and veggies and dip tend to go over well and will eliminate any guilt if the only other food you have that derived from a vegetable is chips. (See Crudité Cups with Parsley Hummus, page 32—they're perfect for kids too!). If there's going to be a lot of running around, pitchers of water and a stack of glasses will keep kids hydrated—add a few strawberries or slices of orange to make it more interesting and juice-like. Beyond that, I like to stick to the easy and cheesy—perhaps pizza or gooey mac & cheese—and something special and memorable that my son will be excited to share with his friends, like the cookie pizza on page 128 or homemade s'mores—with marshmallows roasted in the oven if you don't have a fire pit.—JVR

PERFECT POPCORN

There's no need to buy bags of microwave popcorn to satisfy little snackers; regular kernels can be popped in a plain paper lunch bag. Simply pour about ⅓ cup (80 mL) unpopped corn into a brown paper bag, add 1 tsp (5 mL) canola or other vegetable oil and toss it about to coat. Fold the top of the bag over twice—this is enough to keep it closed as it pops—place in the microwave and cook for 2½–3 minutes, just like store-bought microwave popcorn, until the popping slows. Alternatively, pop your corn in a lidded pot on the stovetop; a drizzle of oil in the bottom and a layer of kernels set over medium-high heat is all you need. Shake the pot occasionally to keep it from singeing on the bottom, and once the popcorn is dumped out into a bowl, you can put a pat of butter in the hot pan and it will melt instantly to drizzle over top.

SLOW-COOKER MAC AND CHEESE

A big slow cooker full of gooey macaroni and cheese is perfect to have on hand with a houseful of kids—especially if you're not sure when mealtime will happen. Sticky, cheesy mac is easy to eat on the couch, in a makeshift tent, or wherever they happen to be when hunger strikes.

1 lb (500 g) elbow macaroni, uncooked

1–1½ lb (500–750 g) old cheddar cheese, grated

one 8 oz (240 g) pkg cream cheese, cut into chunks

4 cups (1 L) 2% milk

salt and pepper

pinch freshly grated nutmeg (optional)

- Combine all the ingredients in the bowl of a slow cooker; cover and cook on low for 3–4 hours, removing the lid to give it a stir about once an hour. Serve warm.

Serves 8–10

NUTELLA S'MORES WITH HOMEMADE GRAHAM CRACKERS

These buttery cookie-crackers are delicious enough to nibble plain, but kids will love spreading them with Nutella and sandwiching them with toasted marshmallows. If a campfire isn't part of your plans, you can broil large marshmallows in the oven for a similar effect—with no risk of dropping them in the ashes. This cracker recipe is adapted slightly from a recipe shared by Crosby's Molasses—an essential ingredient in graham crackers (which are really cookies); alternatively, store-bought graham crackers or digestive biscuits will work too.

GRAHAM CRACKERS

1 cup (250 mL) butter, at room temperature

¾ cup (185 mL) brown sugar

2 Tbsp (30 mL) molasses

1 Tbsp (15 mL) milk

1 tsp (5 mL) vanilla

1½ cups (375 mL) all-purpose flour

1 cup (250 mL) whole wheat flour

½ cup (125 mL) wheat germ or oat bran

1 tsp (5 mL) baking soda

½ tsp (2.5 mL) cinnamon

¼ tsp (1 mL) salt

large marshmallows

Nutella, other chocolate-hazelnut spread, or squares of dark chocolate

- In a large bowl, beat the butter and brown sugar until pale and fluffy; beat in the molasses, milk and vanilla. Add the dry ingredients and beat on low speed or stir by hand until you have soft dough. Wrap in plastic or waxed paper and chill for at least 30 minutes.

- Divide the dough into four pieces and roll each piece out between two sheets of parchment paper to about ⅛-inch (0.3 cm) thick. Move the rectangle to a baking sheet, peel off the top layer of parchment, cut into squares or rectangles and freeze until firm.

- Meanwhile, preheat the oven to 350°F (175°C). Remove dough from the freezer, prick all over with a fork and bake for 10 minutes, until golden. If you like, separate the crackers and bake for a few more minutes.

- To make s'mores, place as many marshmallows as you'd like to toast on a parchment-lined baking sheet and place under the broiler for 1–2 minutes (watch them carefully so that they don't burn)—meanwhile, spread graham crackers with Nutella or place a piece of chocolate on them, top with a still-warm toasted marshmallow, and top with another graham cracker.

Serves lots

OVERNIGHT BERRY CHEESECAKE FRENCH TOAST

If the kids are up late and you find yourself with extra hours to kill before bed, you may as well get breakfast ready the night before, since everyone will be sleepy in the morning. This cheesecake-esque overnight French toast studded with tart berries is beautiful coming out of the oven; serve it warm, with maple syrup.

8 large eggs

1½ cups (375 mL) milk

¼ cup (60 mL) maple syrup

1 tsp (5 mL) vanilla

pinch salt

4 oz (120 g) cream cheese, at room temperature

1–2 Tbsp (15–30 mL) sugar or maple syrup

half a big loaf of crusty bread, cut into cubes

2 cups (500 mL) fresh or frozen raspberries, blackberries, blueberries or a combination

- In a large bowl, whisk together the eggs, milk, maple syrup, vanilla and salt. In a small dish, stir together the cream cheese and sugar.

- Cut or tear the bread into cubes and place in a buttered casserole dish, stopping halfway to add a few dollops of the cream cheese mixture and a handful of blueberries. Add the rest of the bread and scatter with blueberries. Top with blobs of the remaining cream cheese.

- Pour the egg mixture evenly over top; cover with plastic wrap and refrigerate overnight.

- Remove from the fridge about 30 minutes before baking, as you preheat the oven to 350°F (175°C). Bake for 30 minutes, until golden and set. Serve warm, with maple syrup.

Serves 8

ACKNOWLEDGEMENTS

JAN SCOTT

Writing this book was an absolute labour of love, as well as a dream come true, and it wouldn't have been possible without the helping hands and support of the following people:

TO JULIE There are no boundaries to your generosity, and I'm incredibly grateful for your encouragement, advice and friendship, but most of all, I feel pretty lucky that you thought it would be a good idea for us to write a book together. Thank you.

TO WHITECAP Special thanks to Jesse and Jeffrey, for believing in our project from the beginning, and for helping to turn our idea into a published piece of work.

TO BERNARDIN Thank you for being so eager to work with us and for the generous jar donations.

TO THE FAMILY BITES COMMUNITY Thank you for taking the time to read, and for the many thoughtful notes, comments and copious amounts of encouragement. I continue to be amazed that my simple dinners, entertaining ideas and family anecdotes are of interest to you, but boy, am I ever glad they are. Thank you, thank you, thank you!

TO THE GIRLS AT YORKSHIRE PUDDING For hiring me all those years ago, and teaching me so much of what I know.

TO BETH, TESS AND SHANNON Dear friends, recipe testers and bearers of the best advice . . . thank you for cooking your way through the pages of this book, and providing real, honest feedback. I couldn't have done this without you.

TO "THE GATHERERS" Nadine Strople, Ron and Tami Strople, Bill and Pat Scott, Beth and Peter Kostopoulos, Dan and Sharon Scott, Ryan and Jenn Scott, and the little people who accompany you to our many meals (even if they aren't crazy about what's on the menu): Samantha, Katie, Brandon, Tristan, Ally, Thomas, Will and James. I adore you all, and am so thankful that you willingly crowd around my table as frequently as you do.

TO BEN AND JACKSON For so very much, not the least of which is your hearty appetites and eagerness to eat most of what I make. Thank you for being taste testers and for letting me write about you, even when you didn't really want me to, but most of all, thank you for being my dinner dates every night. Life is a delicious adventure because of the two of you, and I love you tremendously.

TO ROB The single greatest moment of my life was the day you walked into it, and everything I have valued since has been given to me by you. I hold you responsible for pretty much every great thing that has happened to me, and I'm amazed that you continue to show me every single day what love is, while asking for nothing in return. Of the many things I'm truly thankful for, seeing your face across the table every day ranks among the highest.

JULIE

Huge thanks to Jan for her never ending insight and advice, for being such a great friend and collaborator, and for dreaming up the concept of *Gatherings*! And as always, thanks to my family, friends and those who join me on *Dinner with Julie*—I'm so grateful for all the amazing and inspiring people in my life. To all who have been there to cheer me on, offered their help or lent their support in so many ways over the years—thank you!

INDEX